Shelly Pagliai

a SIMPLE *life*

QUILTS INSPIRED BY THE '50s

Kansas City Star Quilts Block of the Month

CW00665433

Text copyright © 2016 by Shelly Pagliai
Photography and artwork copyright © 2016 by C&T Publishing, Inc.
Publisher: Amy Marson
Creative Director: Gailen Runge
Editor: Deborah Bauer
Technical Editor: Jane Miller
Cover Designer: April Mostek
Book Designer: Heather Lee Shaw
Photographer: Aaron T. Leimkuehler
Illustrator: Eric Sears
Photo Editor: Jo Ann Groves

Published by Kansas City Star Quilts, an imprint of C&T Publishing, Inc., P.O. Box 1456, Lafayette, CA 94549

All rights reserved. No part of this work covered by the copyright hereon may be used in any form or reproduced by any means—graphic, electronic, or mechanical, including photocopying, recording, taping, or information storage and retrieval systems—without written permission from the publisher. The copyrights on individual artworks are retained by the artists as noted in *A Simple Life*. These designs may be used to make items for personal use only and may not be used for the purpose of personal profit. Items created to benefit nonprofit groups, or that will be publicly displayed, must be conspicuously labeled with the following sentence: Designs copyright © 2016 by Shelly Pagliai from the book *A Simple Life* from C&T Publishing, Inc. Permission for all other purposes must be requested in writing from C&T Publishing, Inc.

Attention Copy Shops: Please note the following exception—publisher and author give permission to photocopy pages 14, 68 and 86 – 95 for personal use only.

Attention Teachers: C&T Publishing, Inc., encourages you to use this book as a text for teaching. Contact us at 800-284-1114 or ctpub.com for lesson plans and information about the C&T Creative Troupe.

We take great care to ensure that the information included in our products is accurate and presented in good faith, but no warranty is provided nor are results guaranteed. Having no control over the choices of materials or procedures used, neither the author nor C&T Publishing, Inc., shall have any liability to any person or entity with respect to any loss or damage caused directly or indirectly by the information contained in this book. For your convenience, we post an up-to-date listing of corrections on our website (ctpub.com). If a correction is not already noted, please contact our customer service department at ctinfo@ctpub.com or at P.O. Box 1456, Lafayette, CA 94549.

Trademark (™) and registered trademark (®) names are used throughout this book. Rather than use the symbols with every occurrence of a trademark or registered trademark name, we are using the names only in the editorial fashion and to the benefit of the owner, with no intention of infringement.

Library of Congress Cataloging-in-Publication Data
Pagliai, Shelly
Library of Congress Control Number: 2016932631

A Simple Life: Quilts Inspired by the '50s/ Shelly Pagliai
ISBN (soft cover) 978-1-61745-332-8

Printed in the United States of America
10 9 8 7 6 5 4 3 2 1

Table of Contents

Dedication

To all the women in my family, especially Mildred, Katy, Danna and Wessal
– but most of all, to Hazel Ilene.

And to my Daddy. I'll always love you most.

Acknowledgments

History was never my thing when I was in school, but undertaking this project plunged me full into a new hobby of historical research, genealogy, photo sorting, interviewing, sleuthing and writing. And I had a lot of help.

Most of all I need to thank My Cowboy, who has helped me and put up with me more than I thought any human being capable of, with nary a complaint. Thanks for always knowing what I need even before I do and making me laugh all the time, even when I don't want to.

And a big thanks to the best sister I could have ever hoped for, Katy Kitchen – for hunting and gathering, running errands, expert sleuthing and helping me with the quilts. (Sorry I was wishing you would be a boy when Mama was pregnant with you!)

Special thanks also goes to:
Larry Hyde
Shirley (Jones) Richard
Jane (Day) Wisdom
Barbara Sue (Spencer) Richardson
Peggy (Rector) Cerva
Anita (Frazier) Enyeart
Sue (Britt) Howard
Patricia (Christy) Teter
Ruth Masten
Victoria Findlay Wolfe
Edie McGinnis
Billy Franke

To the nice folks who worked so hard on this book:
Deborah Bauer
Jane Miller
Aaron Leimkuehler
Eric Sears
Heather Shaw

And to these wonderful industry folks:
Jessica and Jeanette at Sew Sweet Quilt Shop, Brunswick, Mo.
Robert Kaufman Fabrics
Moda Fabrics
Camelot Fabrics
Dear Stella Designs
Riley Blake Designs

About the Author

Determined to train me up in the domestic arts that she herself was so dedicated to, my mother taught me to churn butter in a mayonnaise jar, bake a mean pan of brownies, make roses out of Play-Doh and, most of all, to have fun no matter what I was doing. She highly encouraged make-believe, playing dress up, being kind to animals and minding one's manners. She also began teaching me to sew.

My first project, when I was 5 years old, was a flour sack tea towel, with a puppy stamped on it. My crude attempt was nothing to brag about. Before we got very far into those lessons, she passed away, and her mother, my grandmother Mildred, stepped in.

Grandma enrolled me in 4-H sewing classes when I was 8 years old, where I learned how to use a sewing machine and began making my own clothes. When I was 12, my mother's Aunt Charlotte came to visit and brought me a large garbage bag full of all kinds of fabric scraps. And I began to make a quilt.

That first quilt never made it to the finished stage, and I've come a long way since then. I began teaching others to quilt in 1996, and in 1999, Prairie Moon Quilts was born. (prairiemoonquilts.com) I now have my own line of original quilt patterns and kits and do professional machine quilting for other quilters from my home studio in the upstairs of the 1921 farmhouse I share with My Cowboy.

When I'm not busy teaching classes, writing patterns, operating the longarm or creating my own award-winning quilts, you can find me spending time with My Cowboy and all our many animals at home on Prairie Moon Ranch in rural Wien, Mo.

Shelly Pagliai

Playing dress up at age 4.

Dale, on leave from the Army, standing with his family outside the house he grew up in. He is joined by his parents, Salvatore (Rod) Franklin and Lulu Pearl Britt Pagliai; his little sister, Patti; and his brother, Damon.

The Hyde family outside their farmhouse in Callao, Mo.

Hazel and her brothers, Donald (left) and Larry, posed sweetly on the steps of a neighbor's house in Kansas City, where the family lived during World War II.

Hazel's father, Vern Hyde, served in the Navy in World War II.

While on a family vacation to the Ozarks in the early 1960s, Hazel and her two oldest children, Gary and Shelly, take in the sights.

Introduction

When Pearl Harbor was attacked Dec. 7, 1941, the United States was plunged into World War II. My mother, Hazel Ilene Hyde, was 5. Her family moved to Kansas City to live with her father's mother, while he served in the Navy as a security guard.

When the war ended, my mother's family moved back to a farm halfway between the towns of Bevier and Callao, Mo. My grandfather, Vern, ran the farm and worked in Bevier as a mechanic at Gates Garage. Hazel and her brothers, Donald and Larry, attended school in Callao.

On Christmas Eve 1950, Hazel received a little red five-year diary from her parents. She wrote in the book every day for the next few years, noting events on the farm, the fun she had with friends and the news of the day.

From her freshman year in high school, up until the night before her wedding to her sweetheart, Dale Pagliai, Hazel chronicled everyday life in the pages of her little red book. We used her diary entries verbatim in this book.

It's a unique glimpse into the life of a 1950s rural farm girl making her way through her teenage years. It'll make you laugh and make you cry. If you're old enough, it will bring up some great memories of those times.

When Hazel ends her diary Oct. 2, 1954, the night before her wedding, she leaves a sweet message to her future children. The next day, she married Dale, the love of her life. In their tiny five-room rented farmhouse, she busied herself being a housewife while Dale worked for some area farmers.

In 1957, Dale joined the Army and served eight years. Hazel wanted nothing more than to have a large family, and by 1961, when no children had come along yet, she and Dale adopted a baby boy, who was only a few months old. They named him Gary. And Hazel discovered she was pregnant with me.

They settled in Callao in a cute stucco house at the edge of town. Hazel's life joyfully revolved around her husband and children. She gave birth to me in 1962, Darin in 1965 and Katy in 1969.

Sadly, the little family's world was changed forever when Hazel, at the age of 32, passed away suddenly on Feb. 17, 1969. Katy was only 6 days old.

My mother was an accomplished seamstress, making a lot of her own clothing, sewing most of the clothing for her children and crafting items for her home, including quilts. Each of her children has a quilt she made. The seamstress trait is evidently genetic, because both my sister and I are avid quilters.

The quilts in this book were inspired by my mother and her diary entries, and that period of time in the early 1950s when life seemed so much simpler. I hope you enjoy getting to know the teenage Hazel and making the quilts and projects I designed in her honor.

– Shelly Pagliai

The Life of Hazel Ilene, a website

This project is so much more than just a book. When our father gave my sister and me our mother's diary back in 2001, I knew I wanted to do something with it, but it took me awhile to decide what that would be.

In 2009, as a fledgling blogger at Prairie Moon Quilts, I decided that a daily blog would be a great way to share my mother's diary entries. But diary entries alone might be boring. Who would read that?

I'm also, first and foremost, a quilter, so I came up with the idea of hosting an online quilt-along to accompany the diary entries. Quilts and blocks and other projects inspired by my mother and her diary entries would make the blog more useful to my readers.

Since December 2009, every entry in the diary has been posted, along with as much information as I could find about the events Hazel talks about. I've also posted pictures when I have them and recipes as I can find them. I've also written about my interviews with key diary characters. Five online quilt-alongs have been hosted, a myriad of free bonus projects and free tutorials have appeared, and a line of Hazel's Diary patterns has come about.

With this book, nine more projects inspired by Hazel and her life have made it into the world, with the Hazel's Diary quilt the 2015 Kansas City Star Block-of-the-Month quilt, appearing in the Sunday paper.

And there are many more projects and quilt-alongs to come.

If you'd like to join in on any of these projects, or read the entire diary transcript, please visit hazelsdiary.wordpress.com and use the links in the sidebar to navigate.

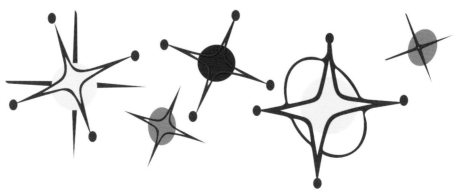

Hazel's Diary Quilt

Finished size: 95" x 95"

Machine pieced, hand appliquéd and machine quilted by Shelly Pagliai

YARDAGE REQUIREMENTS FOR HAZEL'S DIARY QUILT

- 7 yards solid white for background

- 3 ½ yards solid red

- 1 ⅔ yards solid gray

- 1 ¼ yards assorted greens, including prints, polka dots and even a solid or two

- 1 ¼ yards assorted reds, including prints, polka dots, checks and a solid

- 1 yard assorted yellows, including prints and a solid

- 1 yard assorted blue prints, ranging from navy to turquoise to pale blue

- 1 fat eighth assorted black prints, including polka dots

- ⅛ yard assorted gray prints

Save your leftover scraps for the outer border

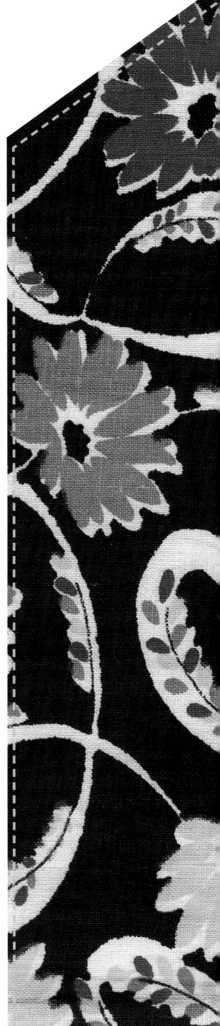

Block 1:
Missouri Farm Life

Our story begins when Hazel makes her very first diary entry.

Jan. 1, 1951
Shirley Jones (a cousin) visited schcool. Got out at 2:30. Ernest Perrin moved to Macon. We went to Charles and Helen Deckers and they were having a Wearever party.

Hazel's family was very social. It was the days of visiting friends and family in person, handwritten letters, walking instead of driving, hard work and good old-fashioned fun. Card parties, school and church events, and going to see movies at the local theaters were some of the highlights.

Jan. 3, 1951
Went to show tonight "Lust for Gold". Really good. 3 tests tomorrow. Its slick today and tonight. Daddy and boys listened to Joe Louis fight. (Joe won) Glenn Ford in show. He's cute. I wore corduroy skirt and white blouse to scholl. I've got to study science. 60 is passing grade.

Most rural homes had had electricity for only a short time, and there were still some that didn't have it yet. In-home telephones, if you had one, operated on a party line. Folks listened to battery-powered radios. Television sets were a rarity.

Jan. 6, 1951
Went to Dave & Ruths tonite. Had popcorn, cokes, and divinity. Reese & Bob wasn't there. Got home at 11:30. Went to Bevier & Callao today. Watched television at Aubreys.

Aubrey Evans owned the hardware store in Bevier, Mo., next door to the garage where Vern worked, and he had the first TV set in town displayed in his store. Kids would gather there after school and line up in front of the TV on pillows on the floor to watch such shows as "Sergeant Preston of the Yukon" and "Sky King."

April 6, 1951
Stayed home tonite. Moms still got her job. She gets over $30 per week. Robert is working for Roy. Daddy got us after school today. Got out at 3:00 oclock. Ervin was at garage. Shirley was at town. Shirley got her hair cut tonite, real short.

Hazel had lots of responsibilities at home, including helping her mother with housework and yardwork, cooking, ironing and keeping an eye on her two younger brothers, Donald and Larry, otherwise known as Buck and Puz. Mildred, Hazel's mother, had a job outside the home, working at a factory. Minimum wage in 1951 was a mere 75 cents an hour. Gas was 27 cents a gallon. And it cost Hazel 3 cents for every letter she mailed.

BLOCK 1: MISSOURI FARM LIFE

BLOCK SIZE: 18" FINISHED

SUPPLY LIST

- 1 – 8" x 13" strip and 1 – 8" x WOF strip white background fabric
- 1 – 4 ½" x 8 ½" strip green polka dot on white
- 1 – 5" x 9 ½" strip red print
- 1 – 5" x 9 ½" strip navy print
- 1 – 7" square yellow print
- 1 – 6" square green print
- 1 – 2" square black print
- 1 – 20" square solid red

CUTTING INSTRUCTIONS / PIECED BLOCK

From the white background fabric, cut:
1 – 7 ¼" square – Cut the square from corner to corner twice on the diagonal to make 4 triangles. (A1)

- 1 – 4 ¾" square (A2)
- 4 – 3 ½" squares (A3)
- 2 – 3 ½" x 12 ½" strips (A4)
- 2 – 3 ½" x 18 ½" strips (A5)

From the green polka dot fabric, cut:

- 2 – 3 ⅞" squares – Cut the squares in half on the diagonal to make 4 triangles. (B1)

From red print, cut:

- 2 – 4 ¼" squares – Cut the squares from corner to corner twice on the diagonal to make 8 triangles. (C1)

From navy print, cut:

- 2 – 4 ¼" squares – Cut the squares from corner to corner twice on the diagonal to make 8 triangles. (D1)

APPLIQUÉ ELEMENTS

From the yellow print, cut:

- 1 each using templates B, C, D, E and F

From the green print, cut:

- 4 pieces using template A

From black print, cut:

- 1 piece using template G

From solid red, cut:

- 1 frame using the frame template on Page 14

ASSEMBLY INSTRUCTIONS

Sew a green polka dot triangle (B1) to two opposite sides of the A2 background square. Press the seams toward the triangles. Sew the two remaining B1 triangles to the other two sides of the square, again pressing seams toward the triangles. The unit should measure 6 ½" square.

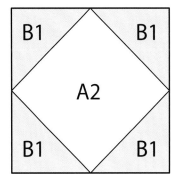

Sew a red C1 triangle to a navy D1 triangle along the short sides. Press seams toward the darker fabric. Make 4 with the red triangle on the left, and 4 with the red triangle on the right.

Sew the units to the A1 triangles as shown. Press the seams away from the A1 triangle. Make 4.

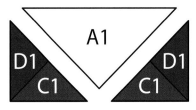

Refer to the diagram below and sew the units into rows. Join the rows to complete the block. It should measure 12 ½".

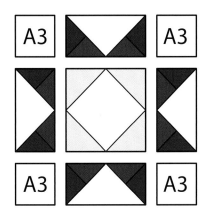

Sew the A4 strips to two opposite sides of the block. Press the seams toward the strips.

Sew the A5 strips to the top and bottom of the block. Press the seams toward the strips. It should now measure 18 ½".

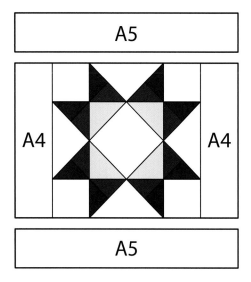

Referring to the placement diagram, and using your preferred method of appliqué, stitch the appliqué pieces to the block in alphabetical order. The red solid block frame is attached using reverse appliqué, or you can use fusible web.

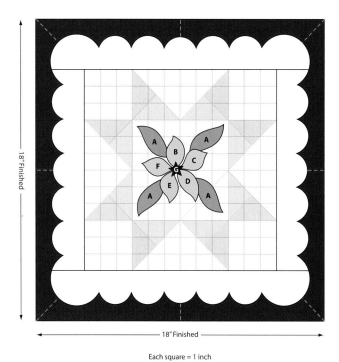

18" Finished

18" Finished

Each square = 1 inch

APPLIQUÉ TEMPLATES ON PAGE 86

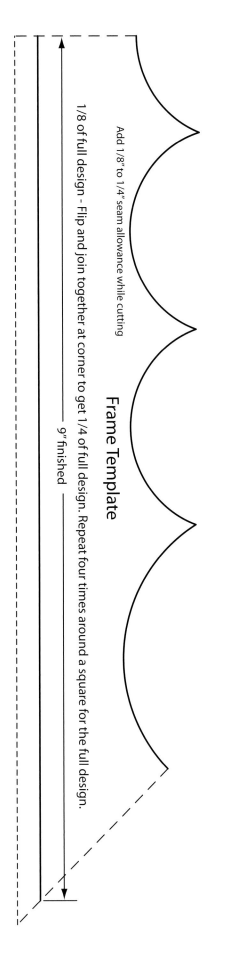

Frame Template

Add 1/8" to 1/4" seam allowance while cutting

1/8 of full design - Flip and join together at corner to get 1/4 of full design. Repeat four times around a square for the full design.

9" finished

Block 2:
Summer of '51

The summer of 1951 unofficially kicked off on Memorial Day weekend, when Lee Wallard won the Indianapolis 500. Four days later, he was severely burned in another race and was forced to retire from racing.

May 30, 1951 – Memorial Day
Went to show tonite, "Stampede,". Real good. We drove out to cemetery before going to show. Reese was here for dinner. (Wait till Mary Ann hears). He worked for Daddy most of day. Listened to Ballgame. Lee Waller won International Speed Race at Indianapolis. I heard part of it.

That summer, Hazel went to Kansas City for a two-week visit with family. She played games with her cousins, ate ice cream, attended carnivals, played miniature golf and visited Fairyland, a popular amusement park.

July 7, 1951
Stayed all day at Maureens. We went downtown all afternoon. Roland & Gradma brought me over to stay with them. Mick, Maureen & Jerry took us to Fairyland tonite. Got a silly picture.

But mostly, it was raining – a lot.
And the Great Flood of 1951 began.

July 12, 1951
Me, Charlotte & Georgie played canasta tonite. We all went to North Town today. Big Mo is out everywhere. I got some presents for the family today. Its rained every day since I been here.

July 13, 1951
The flood up here is awful. Worse than 1903 flood. We stayed up till 2:30 this morning. Northtown may be flooded. Moved people out of Harlins(?). Awful.

July 14, 1951
We all went riding tonite. Can't get to Kansas City. Stopped at a Dari King. Went over to Joyce Martins & Charloote called Maureen. Moma called Grandma.

She's right – it *was* awful. North Kansas City flooded and was among the areas ordered evacuated. The Kansas and Missouri rivers were out of their banks, destroying homes and businesses along the way. Radio announcers gave updates throughout the ordeal, repeating evacuation orders again and again, warning people to get out while they could. Miraculously, in one of the worst catastrophes to ever hit the Kansas City area, only five people died.

Hazel got to go back home to her peaceful life on the farm, far from the flood. She finished out her summer embroidering, crocheting and marveling at how quietly her mother's brand-new automatic washing machine ran.

Aug. 17, 1951

Grandma help me start chrocheting a rug from wool scarfs. I've started another out of cotton, too. Moma got her new washer. Really nice.

Aug. 18, 1951

Grandma gave me a green silk scarf. Its real pretty. We stayed home today & Moma used her new washer. Can't hardly hear it run.

Hazel and her Aunt Maureen had a silly picture taken at Fairyland Park, an amusement park in Kansas City.

BLOCK 2: SUMMER OF '51

MEDALLION SIZE: 36" FINISHED

SUPPLY LIST

- ⅞ yard – white background fabric
- 8" x 20" – Gray solid
- 24 – 2 ¾" x 4 ½" rectangles - assorted prints for flower petals
- 4 – 2" squares – assorted prints for flower centers
- 16 – 2 ½" x 4 ½" rectangles - assorted green prints for large leaves
- 56 – 2" x 3 ¼" rectangles – assorted green prints for small leaves
- 1 – 8" x 18" rectangle green print for vines

CUTTING INSTRUCTIONS

For the piecing:

From white background fabric, cut:
- 8 strips 4 ½" x 18 ½" (A1)
- 4 squares 9 ½" x 9 ½" (A2)

From gray solid, cut:
- 4 strips 1 ½" x 18 ½" (B1)

For the appliqué:

For the vines, from the green print, cut:
- 8 strips on the bias (45° angle) ⅝" wide x 10" long

Or make eight 10" long pieces of ¼" finished bias tape using your favorite method.

From assorted flower petal prints, cut:
- 24 pieces using template B

From assorted flower center prints, cut:
- 4 pieces using template C

From green prints for large leaves, cut:
- 16 pieces using template A

From assorted small leaf prints, cut:
- 56 pieces using template D

ASSEMBLY INSTRUCTIONS

Sew a gray solid B1 strip in between two background A1 strips. Press seams toward the gray strip. This should measure 9 ½" x 18 ½". Make 4.

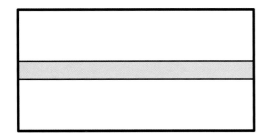

Sew an A2 background square to each end of two of these strip sets. Press seams toward the strip sets.

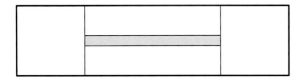

Sew the two remaining strip sets to each side of Block One. Press seams toward the strip sets.

Sew the strips with the squares on the ends to the other two sides of Block One, again pressing seams toward the strip sets. It should now measure 36 ½" square.

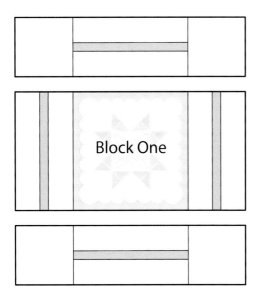

Referring to the placement diagram, and using your preferred method of appliqué, attach the appliqué pieces to the block, beginning with the vines, and then proceeding with the pieces in alphabetical order.

Each square = 1 inch

APPLIQUÉ TEMPLATES ON PAGE 87

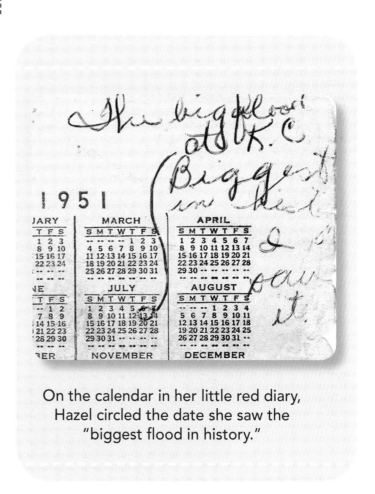

On the calendar in her little red diary, Hazel circled the date she saw the "biggest flood in history."

Block 3:
Canasta

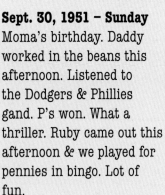

Sept. 30, 1951 – Sunday
Moma's birthday. Daddy worked in the beans this afternoon. Listened to the Dodgers & Phillies gand. P's won. What a thriller. Ruby came out this afternoon & we played for pennies in bingo. Lot of fun.

Without television, Hazel's family listened to the radio a lot and spent time playing games with family and friends.

Men liked horseshoes and golf; women liked croquet and lawn darts. Naturally, games such as hopscotch, tag and hide-and-seek were popular with younger children, but teenagers liked to play hiding games such as Gray Wooley and even a game called murder.

When indoors, they played board games such as checkers, Scrabble and Monopoly – and penny bingo. And everyone, it seemed, played cards. Canasta was a popular card game played in the Hyde family, along with some other variations on traditional rummy, such as Liverpool rummy and books.

The radio had varied programming, including news, sports and talent contests, even some of the same programs that were on TV. Hazel enjoyed sending in requests for songs and dedications (so she could hear her name on the radio), and she loved listening to opera.

Bandleader Horace Heidt had many programs on radio and TV. In 1951, Hazel would have listened to "The Original Youth Opportunity Program," where such stars as Art Carney and Gordon MacRae were discovered.

Dec. 16, 1951 – Sunday
Went to sunday school & church today. It's awful cold out & its snowing. We stayed home tonite & listened to radio. Listened to Horace Heidt finals tonite. A singer won the $5000 dollars.

News about the war was welcomed. The Korean War had been going on for nearly a year and a half at this time, and there were boys from home serving.

Dec. 18, 1951
They are giving out names of U. S. boys in prison camps in Korea. I think its wonderful. The first name was a Major Doujac from Calif. I wrote down about 60 names. Stayed home tonite & listened to radio.

The radio was battery operated and needed to be charged, so the Hyde kids would carry the big, heavy battery down to their grandparent's house about a mile away so that it could be charged on the windmill generator. After a couple hours, they carried it back home, fully charged and ready for all the shows they wanted to listen to.

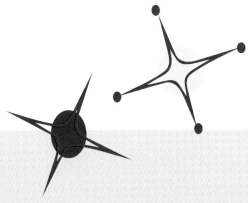

On weekdays, they usually listened to the radio in the late afternoon or early evening before dinner. By Friday, the battery had nearly lost its charge, so they would start the weekend off with a trip to Grandma and Grandpa's to charge the battery all over again.

Gladys and Jim Rector, standing in their yard, 1934.

Hazel's maternal grandmother, Gladys Flossie Hazel Cross Rector. With a knack for making smart business decisions, Gladys helped her husband, Jim, run the Rector farm like a well-oiled machine, while also maintaining her household and raising seven children in the early 1900s. This photo of her in her front yard was taken sometime during World War II.

Hazel's maternal grandparents, Gladys and Jim Rector, celebrating their 40th wedding anniversary, March 1952.

BLOCK 3: CANASTA

BLOCK SIZE: 18" FINISHED

SUPPLY LIST

- 1 – 12" x 13" rectangle and1 – 8" x WOF strip white background fabric
- 1 – 7" x 16 ½" strip yellow print #1
- 1 – 9" square turquoise print
- 1 – 9" square red print
- 1 – 6" x 9" strip green print
- 1 – 4" x 14" strip gray print
- 1 – 1 ½" square yellow print #2
- 1 – 20" square red solid

CUTTING INSTRUCTIONS

Pieced Block

From white background fabric, cut:

- 1 – 6 ⅛" square (A1)
- 1 – 5 ⅜" square – Cut the square in half twice on the diagonal to make a total of 4 triangles. (A2)
- 2 – 4 ⅞" squares – Cut the squares in half once on the diagonal to make a total of 4
- triangles. (A3)
- 2 – 3 ½" x 12 ½" strips (A4)
- 2 – 3 ½" x 18 ½" strips (A5)
- From yellow print #1, cut:
- 4 – 3 ⅜" x 6 ⅛" rectangles (B1)

From turquoise print, cut:

- 4 – 3 ⅜" squares – Draw a diagonal line on the reverse side of each of these squares with a marking pencil. (C1)

From red print, cut:

- 4 – 3 ⅜" squares – Draw a diagonal line on the reverse side of each of these squares with a marking pencil. (D1)

APPLIQUÉ ELEMENTS

From the green print, cut:

- 4 pieces using template A
- From the gray print, cut:
- 4 pieces using template B
- 4 pieces using template C

From yellow print #2, cut:

- 1 piece using template D

From red solid, cut:

- 1 frame using the template on Page 14

ASSEMBLY INSTRUCTIONS

Place a turquoise C1 square on one end of a yellow B1 rectangle, right sides together, with the diagonal line running as shown in the diagram. Stitch on the diagonal line. Press the piece out so that it forms a triangle on one end of the rectangle. Trim the excess fabric out from behind the triangle. Repeat on each of the remaining B1 rectangles.

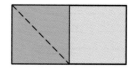 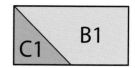

Place a red D1 square on the other end of the yellow B1 rectangle, right sides together, with the diagonal line running as shown in the diagram. Stitch on the diagonal line. Press the piece out so that it forms a triangle on the other end of the rectangle. Trim the excess fabric out from behind the triangle. Repeat on each of the remaining B1 rectangles.

Sew two of these units to two opposite sides of the A1 background square. Make sure the turquoise triangle is next to the center, and the red is on the outer edge. Press seams toward the A1 square.

Sew an A2 triangle to each end of the two remaining rectangle units. Press seams toward the triangles.

Sew these to the two remaining sides of the A1 background square. Press seams away from the center.

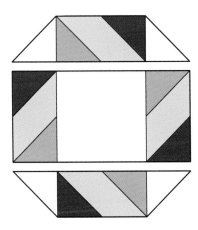

Finally, sew the background A3 triangles onto each corner of the block. (Make sure you're matching the background triangle up against the pieced rectangles, right sides together.) Press seams toward the triangles. The block should measure 12 ½".

Sew the A4 strips to two opposite sides of the block. Press seams toward the strips.

Sew the A5 strips to the two remaining sides. Press seams toward the strips. It should now measure 18 ½".

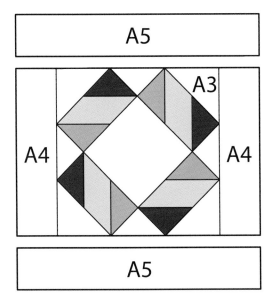

APPLIQUÉ DIRECTIONS

Referring to the placement diagram, and using your preferred method of appliqué, attach the appliqué pieces to the block in alphabetical order. The green leaves extend through the yellow portion of the pieced rectangles. The red solid block frame is attached using reverse appliqué, or can be attached using fusible web.

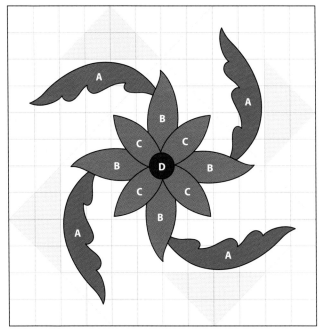

Each square = 1 inch

APPLIQUÉ TEMPLATES ON PAGE 88

21

Block 4:
Coal Miner's Grand-daughter

The Hyde family lived halfway between the small towns of Bevier and Callao in Missouri. Hazel and her brothers attended school in Callao, and their father, Vern, worked at a garage in Bevier. He also worked on their farm, where they raised crops and livestock.

By the early 1950s, coal mining was the big industry in the area. It was Mildred's great-grandfather, Alex Rector, who in 1860 discovered coal just west of town, while digging a well for a farmer.

The discovery spawned an industry that changed the area forever. Bevier's mining district became the greatest in the state. The industry brought in folks from all over who wanted to make a living working in the mines.

On Feb. 12, 1952, Mildred and Vern celebrated their 17th wedding anniversary, and Hazel was busy living a normal teenager's life.

Daydreaming about the boy she recently met:
Jan. 5, 1952
Dave & Ruth came up tonite. I got a letter from Jerry today. Wrote to him, Maureen & Charlotte tonite. Read some old letters, plucked my eyebrows, thought about Dale, & ate doughnuts & apples.

Admiring their new table and chairs:
Jan. 26, 1952
Dave & Ruth came up tonite. We got a new chromium breakfast set (red & gray) this morning. Really pretty. Mom made doughnuts today. I wanted to go to town.

Growing up:
Feb. 6, 1952
Went to show & saw "Follow the Sun", about Ben Hogan, golfer. Oh it was good. I just loved it. Daddy said tonite, "Before long, Suz, you'll be out on a date every night." I thought, "Yeah, I bet I will." Ha.

Being mad at her brothers:
Feb. 18, 1952
I'm so mad I could bust. Donald & Larry are the biggest old tattletales. Mom was mad at me tonite. I'll be glad when school is out & I'm going to leave this darn hole.

Getting her first high heels:
March 29, 1952
Me, Mom & boys went to Moberly with Ruby & Babs this afternoon. Got my first high heels. I like em. Their black trimmed in white. Got my new spring coat, too. Its pale green. We went to Daves & Ruths tonite. I'm so tired I could drop.

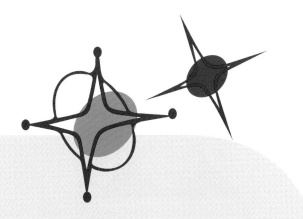

And putting up with drama with friends:

April 14, 1952

I am so mad tonite that I could just bust wide open right now. I'm so mad at Mary Ann I could die. I probably won't be mad tomorrow. Grandpa is going to St. Jo to be operated on. I studied tonite.

Hazel's great-great-grandfather, Alex Rector, who in 1860 discovered coal in Bevier, Mo.

BLOCK 4: COAL MINER'S GRANDDAUGHTER

BLOCK SIZE: 18" FINISHED

SUPPLY LIST

- 1 – 8" x 17" rectangle and 1 8" x WOF strip white background fabric:
- 1 – 4" square red polka dot on white
- 1 – 6" x 12" rectangle black and yellow print
- 1 – 6" square yellow solid
- 1 – 7" square red print #1
- 1 – 5" x 7" rectangle large green polka dot
- 1 – 7" square red print #2
- 1 – 3" square black print
- 1 – 1 ½" square small green polka dot
- 1 – 20" square red solid

CUTTING INSTRUCTIONS

Pieced Block

From white background fabric, cut:

- 1 – 6 ⅛" square (A1)
- 2 – 4 ⅞" squares – Cut the squares in half once on the diagonal to make a total of 4 triangles. (A2)
- 4 – 2 ⅞" squares – Cut the squares in half once on the diagonal to make a total of 8 triangles. (A3)
- 2 – 3 ½" x 12 1/2" strips (A4)
- 2 – 3 ½" x 18 1/2" strips (A5)

From red polka dot, cut:

- 4 – 1 ⅜" squares – Draw a diagonal line on the back of each of the squares with a marking pencil. (B1)

From black and yellow print, cut:

- 1 – 5 ¼" square – Cut the square in half twice on the diagonal to make 4 triangles. (C1)
- 4 – 2 ⅞" squares – Cut the squares in half once on the diagonal to make a total of 8 triangles. (C2)

From yellow solid, cut:

- 4 – 2 ½" squares (D1)
- From red print #1, cut:
- 4 – 2 ⅞" squares – Cut the squares in half once on the diagonal to make a total of 8 triangles (E1)

APPLIQUÉ ELEMENTS

From large green polka dot, cut:

- 4 pieces using template A

From red print #2, cut:

- 4 pieces using template B

From black print, cut:

- 1 piece using template C

From small green polka dot, cut:

- 1 piece using template D

From red solid, cut:

- 1 frame using the template on Page 14

ASSEMBLY INSTRUCTIONS

Place a red polka dot square (B1) on one corner of the A1 background square, right sides together, with the diagonal line running across the corner. Stitch on the diagonal line. Press the piece out so it forms a triangle in the corner of the square. Trim the excess fabric out from behind the triangle. Repeat on each of the remaining corners.

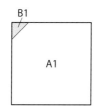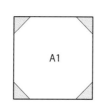

Sew a black/yellow C2 triangle to a solid yellow D1 square as shown. Press seam toward the triangle. Sew another C2 triangle to the adjoining side to make a larger triangle. Press seam toward the triangle. Make 4.

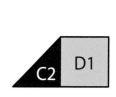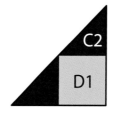

Sew two of these units to opposite sides of the A1 background square. Press seams away from the center. Sew the other two units to the two remaining sides of the A1 square, again pressing seams away from center. This unit should measure 8 ½".

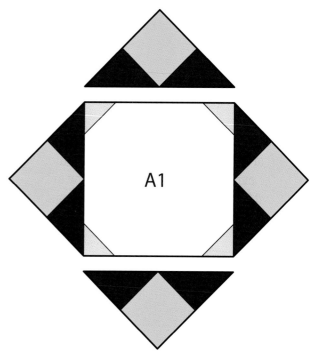

Sew an A3 background triangle to one short side of a C1 triangle, as shown. Sew another A3 background triangle to the other short side. Press seams toward the triangles. Make 4.

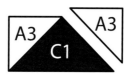

Sew a red E1 triangle to each end of each of these units, making sure to turn them as shown. Press seams toward the red triangles. Make 4.

Sew these to each side of the block center. Press seams away from center.

Sew the background A2 triangles onto each corner of the block. (Make sure you're matching the background triangle up against the red triangles, right sides together.) Press seams away from center. The block should measure 12 ½".

Sew the A4 strips to two opposite sides of the block. Press seams toward the strips.

Sew the A5 strips to the two remaining sides. Press seams toward the strips.

It should now measure 18 ½".

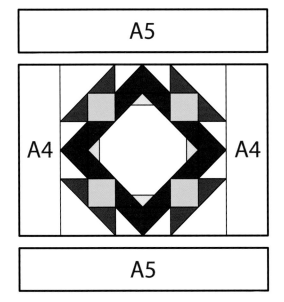

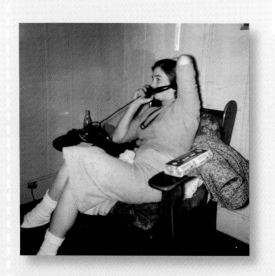

Hazel on the phone at home, no doubt getting all the latest gossip. Note the bottle of Coke on the end table.

Refer to the placement diagram, and using your preferred method of appliqué, attach the appliqué pieces to the block in alphabetical order. The red solid block frame is attached using reverse appliqué, or can be attached using fusible web.

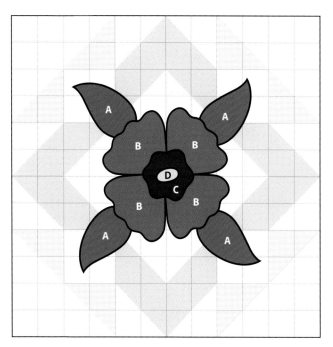

Each square = 1 inch

APPLIQUÉ TEMPLATES ON PAGE 89

Block 5:
Corn and Beans and Other Things

June 11, 1952
Golly, its roasting here. Was up in the 90s today. Got 2 letters from Dale, & Mary A tonite. The sweats running off of me like water in a faucet. Korean war is still going on like always.

The Korean War began June 25, 1950, when troops from Communist-ruled North Korea invaded South Korea. Although truce talks were well underway by the summer of 1952, agreement could not be reached, so the fighting continued.

July 10, 1952
Wrote to Minnie tonite. We stayed home. I didn't do anything but work today. The Republican Convention is going on in Chicago now. I don't feel too awful good.

Dwight D. Eisenhower was the Republican presidential nominee. Part of the party's platform was ending the Korean War. Truce talks did not resume until April 1953, and the fighting finally ended when an armistice agreement was signed July 27, 1953.

Aug. 12, 1952
Me & Lu went skating tonite. I'm dead. We went to Callao, saw Opal, Della, Lorretta & I don't know who all. Billy Ward died today. Me & Lu took some pictures. We read & cleaned house this morning.

Billy Ward, a local boy, had just returned home in May after serving nine months in the Army in the Korean War. He was critically injured in a vehicle accident on Aug. 4. At the time of the accident, he was stationed at Camp Breckenridge, Ky., where he was an instructor.

Despite the grim national news, Hazel's life went on as usual. August was the time of the annual Bevier (Missouri) Homecoming, which she never missed.

Aug. 22, 1952
Dale came up tonite & we went to Homecoming. Won a bunch of dishes & stuff. We took his folks & Patti home, then we came back & rode the rock-o-plane & ferris wheel (Oh!) Then he brought me home. He brought me an autograph bk. from Okla. I love it. Me, & Maureen played tennis at Macon today.

Aug. 21, 1952, was the kickoff of the 19th annual Bevier Homecoming. It began with a big parade at 1:30 p.m. The evening's entertainment included a band concert, vocal and accordion selections, baton twirling, a girls revue, and a unique aerial act. "Sky Man: America's Greatest Flying Act — featuring death-defying thrills in mid air. They will perform twice daily — AFTERNOON and NIGHT."

Hazel seemed more interested in the carnival portion of homecoming, riding the rides and playing the games for prizes. Yvonne Jones, Hazel's cousin, was crowned the 1952 homecoming queen.

BLOCK 5: CORN AND BEANS AND OTHER THINGS

BLOCK SIZE: 18" FINISHED

SUPPLY LIST

- 1 – 17" square and 1 – 8" x WOF strip white background fabric
- 1 – 7" x 13" rectangle red print
- 1 – 7" x 13" rectangle yellow print
- 1 – 3" x 4" rectangle green print
- 1 – 6 ½" square blue print
- 1 – 1 ¾" square black print
- 1 – 20" square red solid

CUTTING INSTRUCTIONS

Pieced Block

From white background fabric, cut:

- 1 – 4 ½" square (A1)
- 14 – 2 ⅞" squares – Draw a diagonal line from corner to corner on the reverse of each of the squares with a marking pencil. (A2)
- 4 – 2 ½" squares (A3)
- 2 – 3 ½" x 12 ½" rectangles (A4)
- 2 – 3 ½" x 18 ½" rectangles (A5)

From red print, cut:

- 7 – 2 ⅞" squares (B1)

From yellow print, cut:

- 7 – 2 ⅞" squares (C1)

APPLIQUÉ ELEMENTS

From green print, cut:

- 2 leaves using template A

From blue print, cut:

- 6 petals using template B

From black print, cut:

- 1 circles using template C

From red solid, cut:

- 1 frame using the template on Page 14

ASSEMBLY INSTRUCTIONS

Match a red B1 square up with an A2 background square, right sides together, with the background square on top so you can see the drawn line. Stitch ¼" on each side of the drawn line, then cut apart on the drawn line. Press seams toward the print fabric. You will have two units that should each measure 2 1/2" square. Repeat for the rest of the B1 squares, and for the C1 squares. You should have 14 of each color.

Lay out two of the B1/A2 units along with two of the C1/A2 units as shown. Sew them together into pairs, pressing seams in opposite directions. Sew the pairs together to make the unit. Make 2.

Lay out two more of the B1/A2 units along with two more of the C1/A2 units as shown (noting that the positions have switched for this set). Sew them together into pairs, pressing seams in opposite directions. Sew the pairs together to make the unit. Make 2.

Lay out three of the B1/A2 units along with an A3 background square, making sure you have them turned as shown. Sew them together into pairs, pressing seams in opposite directions. Sew the pairs together to make the unit. Make 2 using B1/A2 units, and make 2 using the C1/A2 units.

Lay all the units out, along with the A1 background square, making sure you have them in the correct positions, and turned as shown.

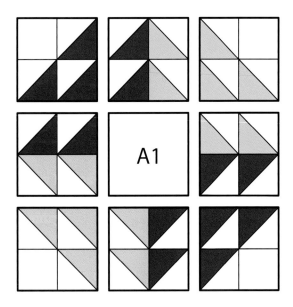

Join the units into rows.

Join the rows to complete the block. It should measure 12 ½".

Sew the A4 strips to two opposite sides of the block. Press seams toward the strips.

Sew the A5 strips to the two remaining sides. Press seams toward the strips.

It should now measure 18 ½".

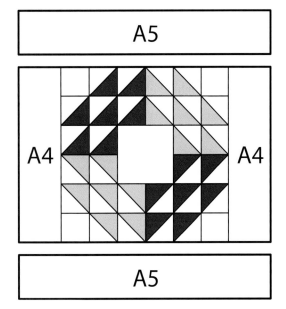

Refer to the placement diagram, and use your preferred method of appliqué to stitch the appliqué pieces to the block in alphabetical order. The appliqué pieces overlap some of the colored patches in the block. The red solid block frame is attached using reverse appliqué, or can be attached using fusible web.

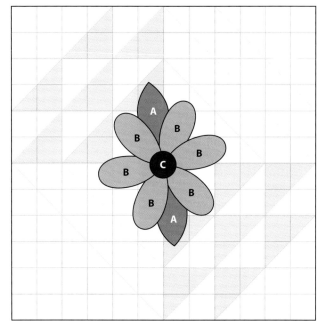

Each square = 1 inch

APPLIQUÉ TEMPLATES ON PAGE 90

Block 6:
Best. Christmas. Ever.

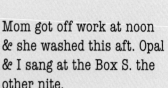

In June 1952, plans were announced to build a drive-in theater in Macon, Mo. It opened four months later.

Oct. 2, 1952

Stayed home tonite & studied. Tomorrow nite a B.B. game with ~~New Cambria~~ Ethel at Callao. The new drive-in is open at Macon. Dale says we are going sometime. Good. We are also going skating, too.

H.P. and O.M. Arnold, an uncle and nephew, built the Macon Drive-in Theater. Dan and Iris Arnold took it over in 1975; they ran it until a tornado destroyed the screen in 2004. They did not rebuild.

The drive-in had a brief first season, but the next spring, many of Hazel's diary entries begin: "Dale came up tonite & we went to the drive in." A month after the drive-in opened, the 1952 presidential election took place.

Nov. 4, 1952

I wrote to Dale today & told him I was sorry. I am, too. Him & Donald W. are getting to be pretty good friends. B.B. game at Atlanta tonite, but I didn't go. Got our class rings today. Today is presidental election.

Nov. 7, 1952

I've felt kind of dazed all day. Oh, golly. Esienhower is our new president – good. We stayed home tonite.

Mom got off work at noon & she washed this aft. Opal & I sang at the Box S. the other nite.

Dwight D. Eisenhower defeated Adlai Stevenson in a landslide. Richard M. Nixon was Eisenhower's running mate. Later that month, the Hydes traveled to Kansas City to celebrate Thanksgiving with family.

Nov. 27, 1952

Thanksgiving – Left for K.C. this morn at 6: oclock. Went to Charlottes for the dinner. Grandma & Roland was there. Went back to G's. this eve & then us kids went home with Mick.

And then the Christmas spirit gripped Hazel. On Dec. 1, 1952, she wrote: "I'm glad December has finally arrived. It gets to seem more like Christmas every day."

She spent December playing games with her brothers, shopping, wrapping Christmas presents and listening to the radio. Her gift for Dale was "a jug of Seaforth mens cologne."

Dec. 21, 1952

Sun. – Dale came up today & brought Patti (his little sister). She is a little doll. She cried when they left cause Dale would'nt take his present. He brought me a great big box. I'm dying to know whats in it. Ruby gave M. a perm. today.

Dec. 24, 1952

Christmas Eve again & it was wonderful this year. Got everything I wanted but a watch band. Dale got me dresser lamps, real cute. We (family & I) went to show & came home unwrapped gifts. Teachers gave H.S. kids a skate party.

Dec. 25, 1952

We went to Gramps & Grammys this aft. & visited. Ruby & Babs stopped by & I stayed & went home with them. They brought me out later. This is the best Christmas ever.

The Macon Drive-in Theater in Macon, Mo., owned and operated by the Arnold family, opened for business Oct. 1, 1952. Photo courtesy Billy Franke.

The Hyde family Christmas tree. Mildred put up this aluminum Christmas tree every Christmas for decades. A lamp with a spinning color wheel projector made the tree turn colors.

BLOCK 6: BEST. CHRISTMAS. EVER.

BLOCK SIZE: 18" FINISHED

SUPPLY LIST

- 1 – 12" x 18" rectangle and 1 strip 8" x WOF white background fabric
- 1 – 4 ½" square red check
- 1 – 6 ½" x 12" rectangle green print
- 1 – 6 ½" square red print #1
- 1 – 7" x 14" rectangle red print #2
- 1 – 2" square yellow print
- 1 – 1 ¼" square black print
- 1 – 20" square red solid

CUTTING INSTRUCTIONS

Pieced Block:

From white background fabric, cut:

- 1 – 4 ½" square (A1)
- 2 – 5 ¼" squares – Cut these squares in half twice on the diagonal to make a total of 8 triangles. (A2)
- 2 – 3 ¼" squares – Cut these squares in half twice on the diagonal to make a total of 8 triangles. (A3)
- 8 – 2 ½" squares (A4)
- 2 – 3 ½" x 12 ½" rectangles (A5)
- 2 – 3 ½" x 18 ½" rectangles (A6)

From red check, cut:

- 4 – 1 ⅞" squares (B1)

From green print, cut:

- 1 – 5 ¼" square – Cut this square in half twice on the diagonal to make a total of 4 triangles. (C1)
- 4 – 2 ⅞" squares – Cut these squares in half once on the diagonal to make a total of 8 triangles. (C2)
- From red print #1, cut:
- 4 – 2 ⅞" squares – Cut these squares in half once on the diagonal to make a total of 8 triangles. (D1)

APPLIQUÉ ELEMENTS

From red print #2, cut:

- 1 of each flower petal using templates A and B

From yellow print, cut:

- 1 star using template C

From black print, cut:

- 1 circle using template D

From red solid, cut:

- 1 block frame using the template on Page 14

ASSEMBLY INSTRUCTIONS

Sew the short side of an A3 triangle to one side of a B1 red check square as shown. Press seam toward the triangles. Sew another A3 triangle to an adjoining side, making sure you have it turned correctly, again pressing seams toward the triangle. Make 4.

Sew a green C2 triangle to this unit. Press seam toward the green triangle. Sew another C2 triangle to the other side as shown, again pressing the seam toward the triangle. Make 4.

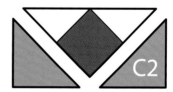

Sew two of these units to the sides of the A1 background square. Press seams toward the A1 square. Sew an A4 background square to each end of the two remaining units. Press seams toward the squares. Sew these to the other two sides of the A1 square.

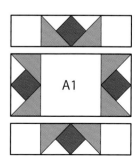

Sew an A2 background triangle to each of the two short sides of a green C1 triangle as shown. Press seams toward the A2 triangles. Sew a red D1 triangle to each end of this unit. Press seams toward the red triangles. Make 4.

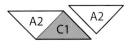 

Sew two of these units to the sides of the block. Press seams away from center. Sew an A4 background square to each end of the two remaining units. Press seams toward the squares. Sew these to the remaining sides of the block, again pressing seams away from center. The block should measure 12 ½".

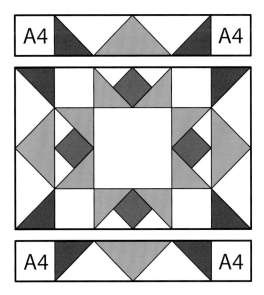

Sew the A5 strips to two opposite sides of the block. Press seams toward the strips.

Sew the A6 strips to the two remaining sides. Press seams toward the strips.

It should now measure 18 ½".

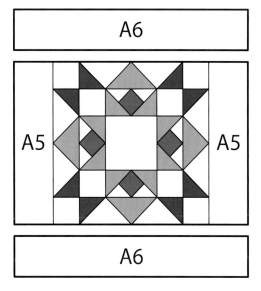

Referring to the placement diagram, and using your preferred method of appliqué, stitch the appliqué pieces to the block in alphabetical order. The red solid block frame is sewn in place using reverse appliqué, or can be attached using fusible web.

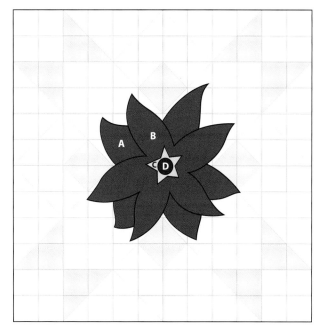

Each square = 1 inch

APPLIQUÉ TEMPLATES ON PAGE 91

Block 7:
Aunt Ruby's Choice

In early 1953, Hazel was 16 years old, interested in boys, very social and beginning to think about what she wanted to do with her life. Some of the careers she contemplated included being a nun (even though she's not Catholic), becoming a Navy nurse or flying the friendly skies as a stewardess.

Feb. 24, 1953
Me & Donna skipped school this aft. & we went to Macon for Donna to hunt for a job. Went by hospital & saw Shirley & Lee's baby (Stephen Glen). I'd love to work there. We stopped by Rubys & told her what we did. Went to Atl. to see Jr. Hi play tonite.

Ruby Rector Spencer, Hazel's aunt on her mother's side, played a prominent role in Hazel's life and is frequently mentioned in the diary. Aunt Ruby was an excellent cook, a wonderful hostess, a kind and generous lady, and a very funny and fun-loving person.

Aunt Ruby was the one Hazel could confess to about such things as skipping school. While Hazel's mother was more strict, Aunt Ruby probably considered Hazel's truancy amusing, and Hazel's secrets were always safe with her.

Outside of Hazel's little world, bigger things were happening. On March 1, 1953, Joseph Stalin, Soviet dictator since 1929, suffered a stroke.

March 4, 1953
Didn't go to school today cause of snow. Judy called tonite & Donna called me at noon. Joseph Stalin, leader of communism in Russia, is about to die. Mom & Dad go to bed with the chicks any more.

March 5, 1953
Stalin died today about 12:30. Dale came up tonite & we went to show at Macon. Saw Della & Harold. Also Damon, Tooter & Mardella Givens. Stopped at Minnies for cup of coffee on way home. Worked on files in office this morn.

While Hazel finds Stalin's death worthy enough to mention in her diary, she's still a typical teenager, learning to drive, participating in school activities, and socializing with all her friends. And her boyfriend takes her to opening night of the new drive-in theater.

April 3, 1953
Dale came up tonite & we went to opening nite of drive-in. I like it. Also stopped by Minnies. He does have his crew-cut. I just love it. I drove home on our road. He doesn't want me to be a nurse.

April 23, 1953
Last nite of our play. Went off pretty good. Afterwards us (play) kids all went to the Moonwinx & danced. I danced with Bill, Leroy, Bernard, & Donna. I rode with Annette, Donna & Opal. The floor was really slick. Had lots of fun. Its 11:15 now.

BLOCK 7: AUNT RUBY'S CHOICE

BLOCK SIZE: 18" FINISHED

SUPPLY LIST

- 1 – 12" x 14" rectangle and 1 strip 8" x WOF white background fabric
- 1 – 6 ½" x 9 1/2" rectangle red print
- 1 – 10" square black and yellow print
- 1 – 4 ½" x 9" rectangle solid yellow
- 1 – 5" square green print
- 1 – 6" square black print
- 1 – 3" square red and white dot
- 1 – 20" square red solid

CUTTING INSTRUCTIONS

Pieced Block:

From white background fabric, cut:

- 2 – 4 ⅞" squares – Cut the squares in half once on the diagonal to make a total of 4 triangles. (A1)
- 1 – 3 ⅜" square (A2)
- 4 – 2 ⅞" squares – Cut the squares in half once on the diagonal to make a total of 8 triangles. (A3)
- 4 – 2 ½" squares (A4)
- 2 – 3 ½" x 12 1/2" rectangles (A5)
- 2 – 3 ½" x 18 1/2" rectangles (A6)

From red print, cut:

- 6 – 2 ⅞" squares – Cut the squares in half once on the diagonal to make a total of 12 triangles. (B1)
- From black/yellow print, cut:
- 4 – 2 ⅞" squares – Cut the squares in half once on the diagonal to make a total of 8 triangles. (C1)
- 8 – 1 ⅞" squares (C2)

From yellow solid, cut:

- 8 – 1 ⅞" squares (D1)

APPLIQUÉ ELEMENTS

From green print, cut:

- 4 of template A

From black print, cut:

- 1 each of templates B, C, D, E, and F

From red/white dot, cut:

- 1 of template G (I fussy cut mine with a red dot centered in the white.)

From red solid, cut:

- 1 of block frame template on Page 14

ASSEMBLY INSTRUCTIONS

Sew a B1 triangle to two opposite sides of the A2 background square. Press seams toward the triangles. Sew the two remaining B1 triangles to the other two sides of the square, again pressing seams toward the triangles. This unit should measure 4 ½" square.

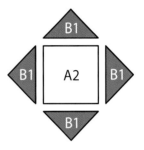

Sew the C2 squares to the D1 squares in pairs. Press seams toward the darker fabric. Make 8 pairs. Sew the pairs together into 4-patches as shown. Press seams to one side. Make 4.

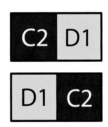

Ruby and her husband, Roy, had one daughter, Barbara Sue. Ruby's holding Barbara Sue in 1945 in the backyard of their home in Bevier, Mo.

Ruby Rector Spencer and her sister, Mildred Rector Hyde (in forefront), after they've finished off a batch of homemade ice cream.

Sew two B1 triangles to two adjoining sides of a 4-patch, making sure to have the 4-patch turned as shown. Press seams toward the triangles. Sew two A3 triangles to the other two sides of the 4-patch, again pressing seams toward the triangles. Make 4. The units should measure 4 ½" square.

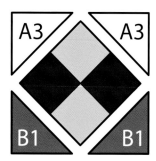

Sew the short side of a C1 triangle to one side of an A4 square as shown. Press the seam toward the triangle. Sew another C1 triangle to the adjoining side of the A4 square to make the unit into a larger triangle. Press seam toward the triangle. Then sew an A1 triangle to this unit to make a larger square. Press seam toward the triangle. This unit should measure 4 ½". Make 4.

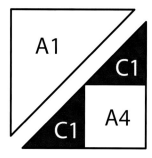

Lay all the units out in rows as shown, making sure you have them turned correctly.

Each square = 1 inch

Join the units into rows.

Join the rows to complete the block. It should measure 12 ½″.

Sew the A5 strips to two opposite sides of the block. Press seams toward the strips.

Sew the A6 strips to the two remaining sides. Press seams toward the strips.

It should now measure 18 ½″.

APPLIQUÉ TEMPLATES ON PAGE 92

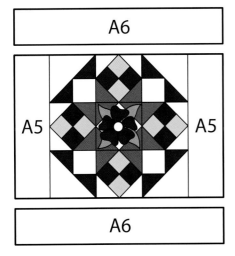

Referring to the placement diagram, and using your preferred method of appliqué, attach the appliqué pieces to the block in alphabetical order. The red solid block frame is attached using reverse appliqué, or can be attached using fusible web.

Block 8:
Domestic Bliss

May 1, 1953

Dale came up tonite & we went to the drive-in. He gave me his class ring to wear & I'm so happy. I love him so awful much. He is getting me red carnations for the banquet.

Hazel and her boy are getting pretty serious – she has his class ring, and they spend an awful lot of time at the drive-in.

May 25, 1953

Stayed home tonite. Daddy worked late so we had supper late. The war is still going on in Korea. They have had a Prisoner exchange. Donna wanted me to go to Macon today. I did'nt.

A prisoner exchange called Operation Little Switch occurred in April and May 1953. It was followed by another exchange later in 1953 called Operation Big Switch. A U.N. commission was formed to take responsibility for the exchange.

Soon after, Hazel marks the first anniversary of her first date with Dale. Now that they're so serious, she's busily working on items for her hope chest.

June 1, 1953

This is a anniversary sort of for me – a year ago today, Dale came up for the first time. It doesn't seem possible we've been going together for a year. Mom & Ruby went to Kirx today. I talked to Judy on phone tonite.

June 2, 1953

I made 8 potholders for my hope chest this aft. I'm also working on my chrocheted rug. Ruby, Barb & Roy came out tonite. Barb is taking dancing lessons. Donna called tonite – wanted me to go swimming. I didn't.

The execution of Julius and Ethel Rosenberg made national news in the summer of 1953. Hazel records her opinion of the incident in her diary.

June 19, 1953

Dale came up tonite & we went to the drive-in. Mom is washing tonite. They electroated the Rosenberg spys tonite at about 6:04 (our time). I think they should have had life sentences but not killed.

The Rosenbergs, who were born and raised in New York City, married in 1939. They were involved in radical political activities. In 1951, they were found guilty of conspiracy to commit espionage for passing information on the atomic bomb to the Soviet Union.

They were sentenced to die in the electric chair. Some thought the Rosenbergs' sentence was too harsh, but all pleas for clemency were rejected. They were executed June 19, 1953, at what was then Sing Sing prison in Ossining, N.Y.

BLOCK 8: DOMESTIC BLISS

BLOCK SIZE: 18" FINISHED

SUPPLY LIST

- 1 – 6" x 10" and 1 – 12" x WOF strip white background fabric
- 1 – 2 ½" x 25" rectangle yellow print
- 1 – 9" x 12" rectangle turquoise print
- 1 – 3 ½" square blue print
- 1 – 5 ½" x 8" rectangle red print
- 1 – 9" x 11" rectangle gray print
- 1 – 20" square red solid

CUTTING INSTRUCTIONS

For the piecing:

From white background fabric, cut:

- 1 – 3 ½" square (A1)
- 4 – 2 ½" squares – Draw a diagonal line on the back side of each square with a marking pencil. (A2)
- 2 – 2" x 9 ½" rectangles (A3)
- 6 – 2" x 6 ½" rectangles (A4)
- 4 – 2" x 5" rectangles (A5)
- 2 – 3 ½" x 12 1/2" rectangles (A6)
- 2 – 3 ½" x 18 1/2" rectangles (A7)

From yellow print, cut:

- 2 – 2" x 3 ½" rectangles (B1)
- 2 – 2" x 6 ½" rectangles (B2)

From turquoise print, cut:

- 4 – 3 ½" squares – Draw a diagonal line on the reverse side of each square with a marking pencil. (C1)
- 8 – 2" squares – Draw a diagonal line on the reverse side of each square with a marking pencil. (C2)

For the appliqué:

From blue print, cut:

- 1 of template A

From red print, cut:

- 1 of template B
- 4 of template C

From gray print, cut:

- 4 of template D
- 4 of template D reversed

From red solid, cut:

- 1 of block frame using the template available on Page 14

ASSEMBLY INSTRUCTIONS

Sew a B1 rectangle to two opposite sides of the A1 background square. Press seams toward the rectangles. Sew the B2 rectangles to the other two sides of the square, again pressing seams toward the rectangles. This unit should measure 6 ½" square.

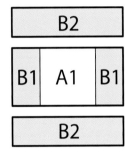

Place an A2 square on one corner of this unit, right sides together, with the diagonal line running across the corner as shown. Stitch on the diagonal line. Press the piece out so that it forms a triangle in the corner of the square. Trim the excess fabric out from behind the triangle. Repeat on each of the other three corners.

Sew an A4 rectangle to two opposite sides of the block. Press seams toward the rectangles. Sew the A3 rectangles to the other two sides of the square, again pressing seams toward the rectangles. The unit should now measure 9 ½" square.

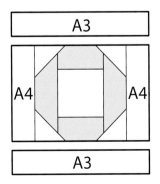

Place a C1 square on one corner of this unit, right sides together, with the diagonal line running across the corner as shown. Stitch on the diagonal line. Press the piece out so that it forms a triangle in the corner of the square. Trim the excess fabric out from behind the triangle. Repeat on each of the other three corners.

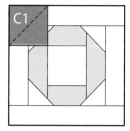 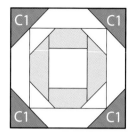

Place a C2 square on one end of an A4 rectangle, right sides together, with the diagonal line running across the corner as shown. Stitch on the diagonal line. Press the piece out so that it forms a triangle in the corner of the square. Trim the excess fabric out from behind the triangle. Make 2. Also make 2 using C2 squares and A5 rectangles.

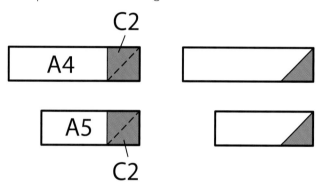

Now repeat this process, but with the triangles on the opposite end. You will have 4 units that look like this:

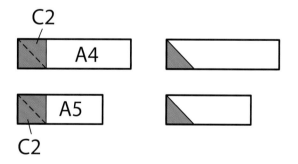

Sew two of the A5/C2 units together as shown. Repeat with the remaining two A5/C2 units. Press seams to one side.

Sew two of the A4/C2 units together as shown.

Repeat with the remaining two A4/C2 units. Press seams to one side.

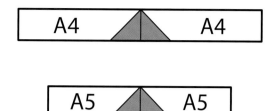

Sew the A5/C2 units to opposite sides of the block, pressing seams away from center.

Sew the A4/C2 units to the other two sides of the block, again pressing seams away from center. The block should measure 12 ½".

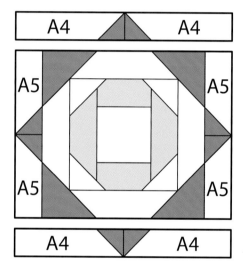

Sew the A6 strips to two opposite sides of the block. Press seams toward the strips.

Sew the A7 strips to the two remaining sides. Press seams toward the strips.

It should now measure 18 ½".

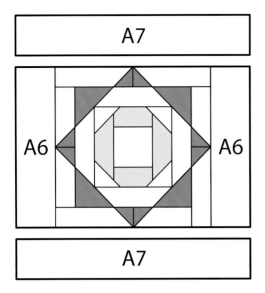

Referring to the placement diagram, and using your preferred method of appliqué, attach the appliqué pieces to the block in alphabetical order. The red solid block frame is attached using reverse appliqué, or can be attached using fusible web.

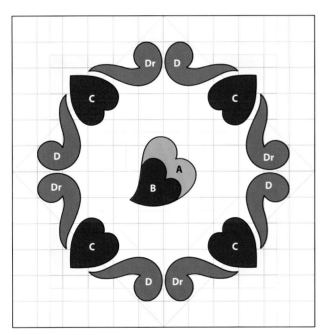

Each square = 1 inch

APPLIQUÉ TEMPLATES ON PAGE 93

Hazel and Dale, on a date. Notice the hoop under Hazel's skirt and the rolled cuffs on Dale's jeans.

Block 9:
Fancy Farm Girl

Sept. 19, 1953
Today I'm 17. Dale came up tonite & brought me a great big fuzzy dog for my bed. It's the cutest thing & I just love it. We went to the drive-in & drove around. Grandma Hyde sent me 2 boxes of pretty stationary. Got my hair cut by Ruth J.

Sept. 21, 1953
We're staying home tonite. Daddy & the boys went to N.C. to get some combine parts & while they were gone Mom & I studied my shorthand. We put a woodstove up in the kitchen tonite. Felt good. I love my hair. Bye

The weather was turning colder, and it was time to bring the stoves back into the house for the winter. Taking the stoves out in the spring provided more space in small kitchens and also brought about the tradition of spring cleaning. Removing the stoves and cleaning up the soot that collected all winter usually caused a flurry of intense cleaning and even putting up new wallpaper each spring.

Oct. 1, 1953
Norman was home from Chicago today & he ask me to go to Kirk. with him to see Bill & Donna but I said no, so he asked Opal & she went. I am Editor-in chief, art editor, girls sports writer on annual staff. New York beat Dodgers first 2 games of World Series.

In a repeat of the 1952 World Series, the 1953 World Series saw the Brooklyn Dodgers facing the Yankees once again. The Yankees were victorious in the seventh game in 1952, but it took just six games for them to triumph over the Dodgers to win the 1953 World Series. It was the fifth World Series Championship in a row for the New York Yankees.

Oct. 10, 1953
Worked all day. Got my history (homework). It took almost all morning. Ruby came out this aft. & I went to Doris' & then to Grandma's with her to get eggs. A few days ago a little boy (Bobby Greenlease) was kidnapped & killed.

The kidnapping of Bobby Greenlease is one of the most famous kidnappings in history. At the time, it led to the largest ransom payout ever – $600,000 – more than half of which was never recovered.

The son of millionaire Robert Greenlease of Mission Hills, Kan., Bobby was taken from his school in Kansas City on the morning of Sept. 28 and murdered by his kidnappers, Carl Austin Hall and Bonnie Brown Heady, almost immediately.

Hall was caught in St. Louis, and Heady was arrested at her home in St. Joseph, Mo., where Bobby's shallow grave was discovered in the backyard. On Dec. 18, 1953, Hall and Heady were executed together in the gas chamber at the Missouri State Penitentiary in Jefferson City.

BLOCK 9: FANCY FARM GIRL

BLOCK SIZE: 18" FINISHED

SUPPLY LIST

- 1 – 10" x 12" rectangle and 1 strip 8" x WOF white background fabric
- 1 – 3 ½" x 6 1/2" rectangle red polka dot on white:
- 1 – 5 ½" square red print
- 1 – 6" x 11" rectangle yellow print #1
- 1 – 6 ½" square and 1 – 3" x 8" rectangle navy print
- 1 – 5" square yellow print #2
- 1 – 20" square red solid

CUTTING INSTRUCTIONS

Pieced Block:

From white background fabric, cut:

- 1 – 5 ¼" square – Cut the square in half twice on the diagonal to make a total of 4 triangles. (A1)
- 1 – 3 ⅜" square (A2)
- 4 – 2 ⅞" squares – Draw a diagonal line on the reverse side of these squares with a marking pencil. (A3)
- 8 – 2 ½" squares (A4)
- 2 – 3 ½" x 12 1/2" rectangles (A5)
- 2 – 3 ½" x 18 1/2" rectangles (A6)

From red/white polka dot, cut:

- 2 – 2 ⅞" squares – Cut these squares in half on the diagonal to make a total of 4 triangles. (B1)
- From red print, cut:
- 1 – 5 ¼" square – Cut the square in half twice on the diagonal to make a total of 4 triangles. (C1)
- From yellow print #1, cut:
- 2 – 5 ¼" squares – Cut the squares in half twice on the diagonal to make a total of 8 triangles. (D1)
- From navy print, cut:
- 4 – 2 ⅞" squares (E1)

APPLIQUÉ ELEMENTS

From navy print, cut:

- 4 of template A

From yellow print #2, cut:

- 5 of template B

From red solid, cut:

- 1 of block frame template on Page 14

ASSEMBLY INSTRUCTIONS

Sew a red polka dot triangle (B1) to two opposite sides of the A2 background square. Press seams toward the triangles. Sew the two remaining B1 triangles to the other two sides of the square, again pressing seams toward the triangles. This unit should measure 4 ½" square.

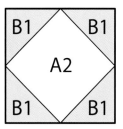

Lay a C1, an A1, and two D1 triangles out as shown. Sew them together as pairs, then join the pairs to make a larger square. This unit should measure 4 ½". Make 4 like this.

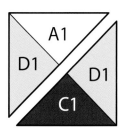

Match up a navy E1 square with an A3 background square. Place the squares together with right sides facing with the background square on top. (You will need to be able to see the drawn line as you sew.) Stitch ¼" on each side of the line, then cut apart on the line. Press seams toward the print fabric. You will have two units that should each measure 2 ½" square. Repeat for the rest of the E1 squares, for a total of 8 of these units.

Arrange two of the E1/A3 units as shown with two A4 background squares. Make sure you have them turned correctly, and sew them together in pairs. Press seams toward the squares. Join the pairs together to complete the unit. This unit should measure 4 ½". Make 4 of these.

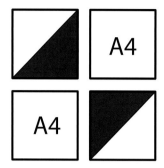

Arrange all the units in the following layout, making sure you have them turned correctly.

Join the units into rows.

Join the rows to complete the block. It should measure 12 ½".

Sew the A5 strips to two opposite sides of the block. Press seams toward the strips.

Sew the A6 strips to the two remaining sides. Press seams toward the strips.

It should now measure 18 ½".

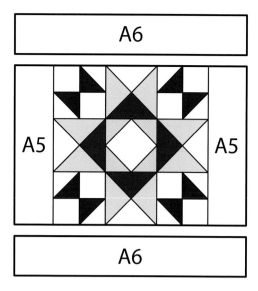

Referring to the placement diagram, and using your preferred method of appliqué, attach the appliqué pieces to the block in alphabetical order. The red solid block frame is attached using reverse appliqué, or can be attached using fusible web.

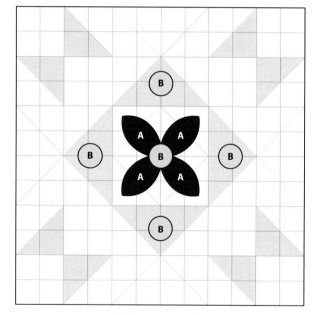

Each square = 1 inch

APPLIQUÉ TEMPLATES ON PAGE 94

Block 10:
Fair Weather

Jan. 11, 1954
Back to school today. I wrote Dale a letter last night and mailed it today. Me, Judy & Charlotte W. (Anita will play) plan to sing "Heart of My Heart" on Quincy T.V. Bye now.

Jan. 23, 1954
Mrs. Christy called today & said she got a letter saying Judy & Charlotte & me sing on T.V. on Feb. 6. Dale & I went to Moberly tonite with Donald & Jane to the show.

Hazel, Judy Anderson and Charlotte Wisdom, accompanied by Anita Frazier on the piano, were invited to sing on "TV Tryouts" on Quincy, Ill., television station W-GEM. They sang "Heart of My Heart."

Feb. 5, 1954
Tomorrow we sing on T.V. I'm not a bit scared. I'm getting ready tonite. Judy called & we talked for a while. Shaved my legs & fixed my hair & its 8:30 now. Hope we can win on T.V.

Feb. 6, 1954
Went to Quincy today & sang on T.V. Did real good & we were'nt scared at all. It was fun. Went shopping & I got bloues & cuff links. Went with Duden & his frat. bro. Got home at 6:30. Judy was with me & her folks came by after her.

Winners were chosen by votes from the audience, submitted by postcard. Hazel's trio got 345 votes, and they were invited back a second time. They appeared on the program Feb. 13 to accept their prizes. Their second singing performance was March 13, when they sang "I Get So Lonely." In the end, another act received more votes for the final win.

March 13, 1954
We girls went to Quincy today for finals in T.V. Tryouts. Duden & Norma E. took us. Had so much fun. I hope we win. Got me a hat & garter belt & had 4 pictures take. I'm dead tired. Ate candy all way home.

March 1, 1954
Stayed home tonite. We T.V. girls sing at Bevier at Congregational church on Fri. aft.noon. There is so much going on I'm almost sick. Some Communists shot up some Senotors today in Wash. D.C.

Four Puerto Rican nationalists, led by Lolita Lebron, 34, entered the Capitol Building and fired 29 shots into the chamber where House members were debating an immigration bill. She screamed "Viva Puerto Rico libre!" ("Long Live a Free Puerto Rico!") and unfurled a Puerto Rican flag as the group opened fire. They were arrested after injuring five congressmen. No one was killed in the attack.

BLOCK 10: FAIR WEATHER

BLOCK SIZE: 18" FINISHED

SUPPLY LIST

- 1 – 12" x 17" rectangle and 1 strip 8" x WOF white background fabric:
- 1 – 10" square yellow print
- 1 – 7" square red print
- 1 – 6" square multicolored print (red, yellow, blue, white)
- 1 – 4" x 10" rectangle green print
- 1 – 7" square navy print
- 1 – 3" x 6" green solid
- 1 – 5" square red solid
- 1 – 20" square red solid

CUTTING INSTRUCTIONS

Pieced Block:

From white background fabric, cut:

- 1 – 4 ½" square (A1)
- 4 – 2 ⅞" squares – Draw a diagonal line on the reverse side of these squares with a marking pencil. (A2)
- 12 – 2 ½" squares – Draw a diagonal line on the reverse side of 8 of these squares with a marking pencil. (A3)
- 2 – 3 ½" x 12 ½" rectangles (A4)
- 2 – 3 ½" x 18 ½" rectangles (A5)

From yellow print, cut:

- 4 – 4 ½" squares (B1)

From red print, cut:

- 4 – 2 ⅞" squares (C1)

From multicolored print, cut:

- 4 – 2 ½" squares (D1)

APPLIQUÉ ELEMENTS

From green print, cut:

- 4 of template A
- 4 of template B

From red solid, cut:

- 1 of template C
- 4 of template F

From navy print, cut:

- 4 of template D

From green solid, cut:

- 4 of template E

From red solid, cut:

- 1 of block frame template on Page 14

ASSEMBLY INSTRUCTIONS

Place an A3 square on one corner of a yellow B1 square, right sides together, with the diagonal line running across the corner as shown. Stitch on the diagonal line. Press the piece out so that it forms a triangle in the corner of the square. Trim the excess fabric out from behind the triangle. Repeat on the other top corner of the B1 square, with the drawn line running as shown. This unit should measure 4 ½" square. Make 4.

Match a red C1 square up with an A2 background square, right sides together, with the background square on top so you can see the drawn line. Stitch ¼" on each side of the drawn line, then cut apart on the drawn line. Press seams toward the print fabric. You will have two units that should each measure 2 ½" square. Repeat for the rest of the C1 squares, for a total of 8 units.

Arrange two of the C1/A2 units as shown with an A3 background square and a D1 square. Make sure you have them turned correctly and in the correct positions, and sew them together in pairs. Press seams toward the squares. Join the pairs together to complete the unit. This unit should measure 4 ½". Make 4.

Arrange all the units and the A1 background square in the following layout, making sure you have them turned correctly.

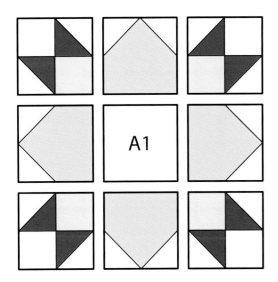

Join the units into rows.

Join the rows to complete the block. It should measure 12 ½".

Sew the A4 strips to two opposite sides of the block. Press seams toward the strips.

Sew the A5 strips to the two remaining sides. Press seams toward the strips.

It should now measure 18 ½".

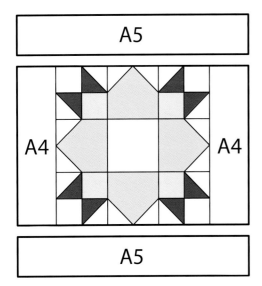

Referring to the placement diagram, and using your preferred method of appliqué, attach the appliqué pieces to the block in alphabetical order. The red solid block frame is attached using reverse appliqué, or can be attached using fusible web.

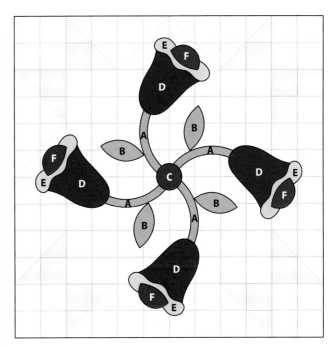

Each square = 1 inch

APPLIQUÉ TEMPLATES ON PAGE 94

A photo ran in the local paper after Hazel and some friends sang on "TV Tryouts" on a Quincy, Ill., television station.

Block 11:
Moonlight and Roses

Hazel's social calendar was full of school activities in spring 1954 as graduation drew near, and she wrote, "Dale told his folks that he's going to give me a ring."

April 16, 1954
Dale came & got me at chuch after Easter Practice. & he gave me my Grad. present – a diamond. I was thrilled to peices. I could have died. Its real pretty & the wedding ring is beautiful. I'm so happy!

It's official: Hazel and Dale are engaged. She writes, "I just love being engaged. Its such a nice feeling." She made herself a "purple princess dress" for the Moonlight and Roses banquet, the first junior/senior banquet to be held in the new school gymnasium, which was finished and dedicated Oct. 11, 1953.

April 23, 1954
Went to banquet tonite – Moonlight & Roses. Was real nice. Afterwards Dale & I went to Moberly with Don & Jane to the Wayside & then out to Reed's Corner. Had fun.

The seniors took a class trip to the Ozarks for four days, doing lots of sightseeing, souvenir shopping and other activities.

May 1, 1954
Went to Branson & Shepherd of the Hills Country this morn & then this aft. came back to Rock-a-way & we rode in a speed boat & me & Don rode a pedalo. Had fun. Ate at Naitos & had Chams party & then bowled, danced & play min. golf.

May 13, 1954
Messed around in town all day – went to Macon with kids & had fun. Tonite was graduation. It was so prety. I got valed. pin & Alpha Phi Sigma admittance. Afterwards Seniors & teachers had a chicken dinner at Johnny & Maggies.

There were seven students in the graduating class of Callao High School that year. Hazel was valedictorian. By June, the summer heat was setting record highs across the country.

June 10, 1954
Staying home again tonite. Mom is gone to a church party. Boy, is it ever hot. I'm going to fix something cold to drink before I go to bed. It was 91° today.

Hazel at her high school graduation, May 13, 1954, at the Callao Christian Church in Callao, Mo.

Goofing around in the Ozarks on the senior class trip, Hazel poses with a shotgun and a whiskey jug while wearing a coonskin cap.

Dale, Hazel, Jane Day and Donald Wisdom in their finery for the Moonlight and Roses banquet.

BLOCK 11: MOONLIGHT AND ROSES

SUPPLY LIST

- 2 ¼ yards white background fabric:
- 1 ⅝ yards gray solid
- 20 – 5" squares various scrappy prints similar to or the same as used in the blocks

CUTTING INSTRUCTIONS

Pieced Block:

From white background fabric, cut:

- 12 – 3 ½" x 26" rectangles (A1)
- 6 – 9" squares – Cut the squares in half once on the diagonal to make a total of 12 triangles. (A2)
- 30 – 4 ⅛" squares – Cut the squares in half twice on the diagonal to make a total of 120 triangles. (A3)

From the scrappy prints, cut:

- 60 – 2 ½" squares (B1)

From gray solid, cut:

- 12 – 4 ½" x 34" rectangles (C1)

ASSEMBLY INSTRUCTIONS

Arrange 10 A3 triangles with five B1 squares in the following arrangement, mixing up the B1 squares for a scrappy look.

Sew them together in diagonal rows, pressing seams toward the squares. Join the rows together to complete the unit, pressing seams to one side.

Locate the center point of the long side of an A2 triangle, and match it up with the center point on the shorter edge of the A3/B1 unit, right sides together. Sew them together, and press the seam toward the A2 triangle.

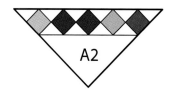

Locate the center point of the long side of an A1 rectangle, and match it up with the center point of the longer edge of the A3/B1 unit, right sides together. Sew them together, and press the seam toward the A1 strip. Repeat and add the C1 rectangle, pressing the seam allowance toward the C1 rectangle.

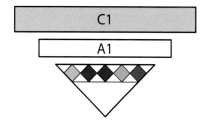

Trim the sides of the unit straight to make a large triangle, using the bottom edges of the unit as a guide. Make 12 of these.

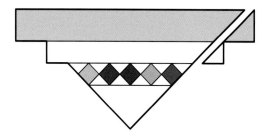

Set 4 of the units aside for now. Sew the remaining 8 units together into pairs as shown. Press seams to one side. Make 4 of these.

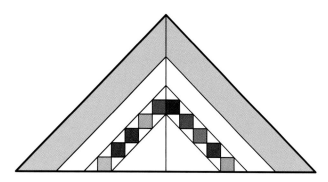

Next, lay out all your previous blocks and your blocks 1 and 2 medallion as shown, making sure the arrangement suits you. Join the blocks in pairs, pressing seams to one side. Sew the pairs of blocks on the sides to the center medallion. Press seams toward the center medallion. Add all the setting triangle units to the layout as shown.

Sew the setting triangles to the ends of the two pairs of blocks that aren't attached to the center yet. Press seams toward the setting triangles. The setting triangles will appear to be too large for the blocks. This is how it should be.

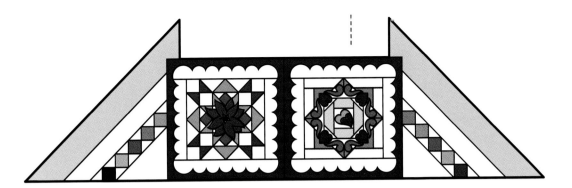

Sew the setting triangle pair to the outer side of each pair, crossing over the portion of the other setting triangles where they stick out. Press seams to one side. Check to see that the gray strip lines up as it should, and that the intersection of the gray strips lies flat, then trim the excess out from behind the setting triangles.

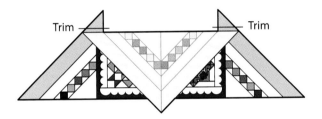

Repeat for the bottom set of blocks and setting triangles. Then join the three sections of blocks together. Finally sew the two remaining pairs of setting triangles onto the corners, checking to make sure everything lines up before trimming the excess out from behind.

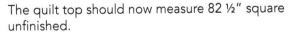

The quilt top should now measure 82 ½" square unfinished.

Block 12:
Happily Ever After

July 13, 1954
Dale came up tonite &
we saw "Three Coins in a
Fountain". Was real good. We
are going to Italy some day.
We have just about got our
farm. (5 room house)

In the sweltering summer of 1954, Hazel is busy
planning her upcoming wedding: "got the bride &
groom for the cake & some satin & lace for the ring
pillow & we saw about some napkins . . . I got my
guest book, plates for reception," and she was relieved
when Dale "liked the same wedding invitation I did."

In August, she set aside wedding planning long
enough to go on a two-week vacation with her entire
family, sightseeing their way out to Washington state
to visit Mildred's sister, Esther, who lived in Tacoma.

Aug. 17, 1954
We're in Custer, S.D. tonite staying at Star Court.
What a day. Went through Badlands and on to Black
Hills. Saw Rushmore Faces. Went on Needles Drive –
saw Needles Eye & Totem Pole. Took lots of pictures.

They "went thro the Bighorns," visited Yellowstone
National Park and "saw Old Faithful . . . erupt."

Other highlights were the redwood trees, San
Francisco, driving through the desert, Las Vegas, the
Salt Lake Temple in Salt Lake City and going "over the
Royal Gorge Bridge."

Once back home, wedding preparations continued.
Dale found them a place to live, and they worked
together getting ready to
move in. The wedding is
set for Oct. 3 at the Bevier
Baptist Church.

Sept. 13, 1954
I could just die. Dave ran
over Tuffy last nite & killed him. I cried till I was
sick. I feel so sorry for Puz. Me, Mom & Ruby went
to Moberly today & I got my wedding gown & veil.
Its absolutely beautiful. White & satin & lacy. Also
got shoes, earrings, strapless bra & other things.
Bye – I'm tired.

On Sept. 19, 1954, Hazel turned 18. Some of her
closest friends hosted a surprise bridal shower for
her.

Sept. 23, 1954
I went up to Judy's tonite to practice on our songs
& my gosh there came a whole bunch of people to
have me a shower. It was wonderful. I got a million
things – crystal, blankets & everything. About
40 there I believe. I saw Dale after it was over. I
thought I'd die.

And finally, everything is ready:

Oct. 2, 1954
Got my hair fixed at Macon today. All K.C. company
is here. We practiced at the church tonite. I guess
everything will be o.k. Tonite I'm ending my diary,
cause I don't want to write anymore after I'm
married. I hope all my children read this & I hope
they have as much fun in their teens as I have.
Bye – Hazel

Hazel and her brothers, Larry and Donald (left), visiting the Badlands in South Dakota, Aug. 17, 1954.

And that's all she wrote. Hazel has ended her diary, the night before her wedding, with a special sweet note to her future children. The wedding did indeed take place, and the story of Hazel and Dale began.

Hazel's brother, Larry, aka Puz, with his little dog, Tuffy, in the summer of 1954, when Larry turned 13.

Mr. and Mrs. Dale Pagliai, Oct. 3, 1954.

BLOCK 12: HAPPILY EVER AFTER
OUTER BORDERS

SUPPLY LIST

- 1 ½ yards white background fabric
- 19 different 10" squares – various scrappy prints similar to or same as what has been used in the blocks
- ¾ yard red solid for binding

CUTTING INSTRUCTIONS

From white background fabric, cut:
- 8 – 2 ¼" x WOF strips (A1)
- 9 – 2 ½" x WOF strips (A2)

From the scrappy prints, cut:
- 472 – 2" squares (B1)

From the red solid, for the binding, cut:
- 10 – 2 ¼" x WOF strips

ASSEMBLY INSTRUCTIONS

Sew two A1 strips together to make one longer strip. From this, cut a length of 82 ½". Sew this strip to one side of the quilt top. Press the seam toward the strip. Repeat on the opposite side of the quilt top.

Sew two more A1 strips together to make one longer strip. From this, cut a length of 86". Sew this strip to the top of the quilt top. Press the seam toward the strip. Repeat on the bottom edge of the quilt top.

A1
82½"

A1
86"

Sew all the B1 squares together into pairs, mixing them up randomly for a scrappy effect. Sew 57 of these pairs together into one long strip. Repeat three more times, so that you have one strip of 57 pairs for each side of the quilt. You should have 8 pairs of B1 squares left over. Sew these into four 4-patches.

Four strips of 57 pairs

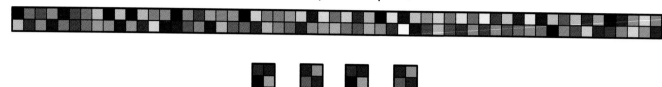

Remaining pairs sewn into four 4-patches

Sew two of the strips of B1 squares to two opposite sides of the quilt, pressing seams toward the quilt center.

Sew the 4-patches to the ends of the two remaining strips of B1 squares, and sew these strips to the two remaining sides of the quilt top. Press seams toward the quilt center.

Two strips of 57 pairs, with 4-patch added to each end.

Sew the four remaining A2 strips together to make one longer strip, and sew the leftover from the strip not used above to the end as well. From this, cut two lengths 95 ½". Sew these strips to the top and bottom of the quilt top. Press the seam toward the strip.

A2
91½"

A2
95½"

Sew five A2 strips together to make one longer strip. From this, cut two lengths 91 ½". Sew these strips to opposite sides of the quilt top. Press the seams toward the strips.

Layer the quilt top with batting and backing. Quilt as desired. After the quilting is complete, square up the quilt and trim away all excess batting and backing. Bind, using the red solid binding strips.

Projects

Dear Diary Quilt

Finished size: 74" x 74"
Pieced and appliquéd by Katy Kitchen
Quilted by Shelly Pagliai

For three years and nine months, Hazel faithfully wrote in her little red diary. As she wrote throughout the years, it was evident that she was growing from a young girl into a mature lady, ready to become a wife and mother. The diary contains 1,371 handwritten entries – what dedication that required!

This quilt, called Dear Diary, is an alternate version of the Hazel's Diary quilt. Dear Diary was pieced and appliquéd by Hazel's youngest daughter, Katy, and features the nine blocks in a straight setting with the wildflower appliqué on them. The appliquéd frames give added definition to the sashing.

When choosing colors for the appliquéd wildflowers, make sure there is good contrast between the pieced block and the flower fabrics, to make the flowers show up well.

SUPPLY LIST

- 5 yards light background fabric for blocks, sashing and borders

- 4 yards green for block frames, corner posts and binding

- 3 fat quarters of each of following colors for blocks and appliqué: Blue, green, yellow, orange, gray

- 4 ½ yards for backing (44/45") or 2 ¼ yards of 90"-wide backing

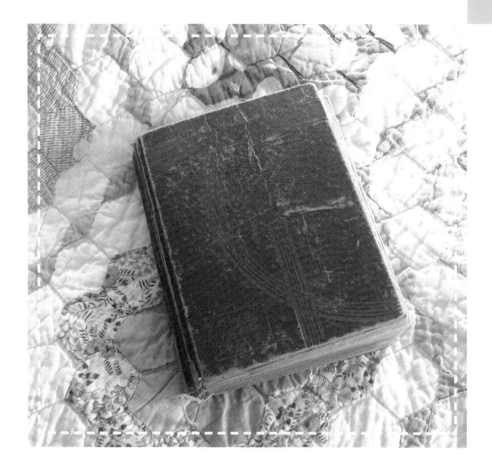

Hazel's little red diary, a Christmas gift from her parents in 1950.

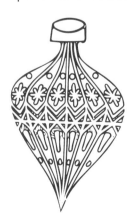

ASSEMBLY INSTRUCTIONS

Make the 9 pieced blocks with appliqué, including the appliquéd frames, according to individual block instructions. See pages 12-47.

CUTTING INSTRUCTIONS FOR SETTING:

From background fabric, cut:

- 24 – 3 ½" x 18 ½" strips for sashing
- 8 – 4 ½" x WOF strips for outer borders

From green, cut:

- 16 – 3 ½" squares for corner posts
- 8 – 2 ¼" x WOF for binding

SETTING ASSEMBLY:

Place the blocks in 3 rows of 3 blocks, in an arrangement that suits you.

Sew a 3 ½" sashing strip in between each pair of blocks, and also at each end of the row.

Press seams toward the sashing strips. Make three rows.

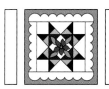 

Using the green corner posts, and the rest of the sashing strips, piece 4 strips like this:

Press seams toward the sashing strips.
Sew these rows in between the rows of blocks.
Piece the outer border strips together in pairs to make longer lengths. Cut two of the lengths to 66 ½". Add these strips to the sides of the quilt.

Cut two more lengths to 74 ½". Add these to the top and bottom of the quilt. Refer to the photo of the quilt for placement.

Woman's Work Quilt

Finished size: 64" x 64"
Made by Shelly Pagliai

In her diary, Hazel mentioned quite often how much ironing she did, and how it could sometimes be an all-day affair. In fact, she mentioned ironing 59 times throughout the diary. Hazel's cousin Shirley told the story of why ironing used to take nearly all day in the early 1950s:

"First, the clothes had to be 'dampened down' which meant sprinkling them with water (a Pepsi bottle with a sprinkler head on a cork jammed into the bottle worked well). Then the clothes had to 'take the dampness' which meant that each item was rolled up as it was sprinkled and the whole lot was wrapped up in a blanket, or plastic, or something to hold the dampness in. After awhile, maybe a few hours, the clothes were evenly wet which made them ready for ironing. We did not dampen towels and underwear but we had to iron it. Can you imagine?!! That – on top of all the dampened stuff – made for quite an ironing day.

"It was easy to scorch the clothes when the iron was too hot or if I left it in one place too long. I have scorched a lot of things in my day!"

Some of the fabrics in this alternate version of the main quilt include motifs such as irons, ironing boards and washing powder, prompting my sister and me to name this quilt after the phrase "A woman's work is never done." Thank goodness for permanent press!

Woman's Work features the same nine blocks in an on-point setting, without the appliqué, and with another little setting block added. Sporting the same outer borders used in the main quilt, this version is made in some of the softer colors that were popular in the early 1950s.

SUPPLY LIST

- Assorted focal and small print fabrics in blue, pink, green, gray, yellow and red to equal 3 ½ yards for blocks and borders.

- 3 ½ yards light background fabric for blocks, setting triangles and borders

- ½ yard for binding

- 4 yards for backing (44/45") or 2 yards of 90"-wide backing

Hazel's cousin, Shirley Jones, happily dancing with a mop at someone's bridal shower. Shirley was a senior in high school at the time.

ASSEMBLY INSTRUCTIONS

Make the 9 pieced blocks, leaving off the 3 ½" framer and appliqué, according to individual block instructions. For the center portion of each block (piece A1), use a focal print fabric instead of plain background fabric. The blocks should measure 12 ½" unfinished. See pages 12-47.

FOR THE SETTING BLOCKS, USE THE FOLLOWING PIECES FROM BLOCK 6 ON PAGE 32:

Piece A1 (cut from a focal print fabric)

Pieces A2, A3 and A4 (cut from background fabric)

Pieces B1 and C2 (cut from prints)

Follow the steps for making Block 6 through the bottom of Page 32, making only the center portion of the block. Make 4.

Each setting block should measure 8 ½" unfinished at this point.

From the background fabric, cut the following pieces:

- 8 rectangles 2 ½" x 8 ½"
- 8 rectangles 2 ½" x 12 ½"

Sew a 2 ½" x 8 ½" rectangle to the sides of each setting block, pressing seams toward the strips.

Sew the 2 ½" x 12 ½" rectangles to the top and bottom of each block, again pressing seams toward the strips.

These blocks should now measure 12 ½" unfinished.

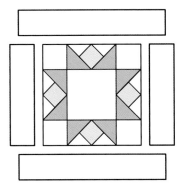

CUTTING INSTRUCTIONS FOR SETTING:

From background fabric, cut:

- For setting triangles, 2 squares 18 ¼"
  Cut these squares in half twice on the diagonal to make 8 triangles

- For corner triangles, 2 squares 9 ½"
  Cut these squares in half once on the diagonal to make 4 triangles

- 6 – 2" x WOF strips for inner border

- 7 – 2 ½" x WOF strips for outer border

From various scraps and leftovers from the blocks, cut:

- 304 – 2" squares for pieced border

From the binding fabric, cut:

- 7 – 2 ¼" x WOF strips

SETTING ASSEMBLY:

Place the blocks in 3 rows of 3 blocks, on point, in an arrangement that suits you. Position the four setting blocks in the empty spaces between the blocks in the middle portion of the quilt.

Position the large setting triangles along the sides to fill in and the four corner triangles at each corner.

Sew the blocks and setting triangles together in diagonal rows, then join the rows together to complete the center portion of the quilt top. Press seams toward the sashing strips.

ADDING THE BORDERS:

Piece three of the 2" inner border strips together to make one long strip. From this, cut two lengths 51 ½". Add these strips to the sides of the quilt.

Piece three more 2" inner border strips together and from it, cut two lengths 54 ½". Add these to the top and bottom of the quilt.

Sew the 2" squares together into random scrappy pairs, then sew the pairs together randomly to make scrappy 4-patches. Make 76 4-patches.

 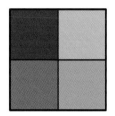

Set the 4-patches together into two long rows of 18 4-patches and two long rows of 20 4-patches.

Sew the rows of 18 4-patches to the sides of the quilt top. Press seams toward the background strips.
Sew the rows of 20 4-patches to the top and bottom, again pressing seams toward the background strips.

Piece the 2 ½" outer border strips together to make one long strip. From this, cut two lengths 60 ½".

Add these strips to the sides of the quilt.

From the long 2 ½" outer border strip, cut two lengths 64 ½". Add these to the top and bottom of the quilt.

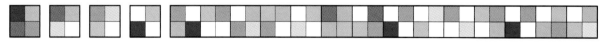

Summer of '51 Tablecloth

Finished size: 47" x 47"
Pieced and appliquéd by Katy Kitchen
Quilted by Shelly Pagliai

The summer of 1951 saw the Great Flood of Kansas City. Although Hazel witnessed the flood herself while visiting with family, she spent most of her summer at home on the farm, helping with gardening and household chores, attending the Bevier (Missouri) Homecoming, eating homemade ice cream, and spending time with friends and family.

It seemed for the most part to be a simple, pleasant summer, filled with normal summertime activities. One of my favorite diary entries from the Summer of '51 is this one, where she tells a funny story about her little brother Larry, aka Puz:

Aug. 20, 1951
Ira's folks is at Grandma's house. It stormed this morning & this evening. I ironed & cleaned house today. Donald was at Ruby's most all day & Momma worked.

Today I made some popcicles & tonite me & buck got one while puz was in bathtub. Puz got in a hurry to get one & was in tub only 2 min. Mom asked him if he took a bath & he said "I washed my face."

Summertime is a time for picnics, and this little tablecloth, inspired by table linens from the 1950s, would put a nice touch on any summer picnic. It features the Summer of '51 applique from the Hazel's Diary quilt. Choose your favorite retro color for your border background to make it all your own.

SUPPLY LIST

- 1¼ yards white solid for background

- 1½ yards aqua solid for borders and binding

For appliqué:

- Red scraps for flower petals

- Yellow scraps for flower centers

- Green scraps for leaves

- Gray for vines

CUTTING INSTRUCTIONS

From white background fabric, cut:

- 1 – 38 ½" square

From border fabric, cut:

- 5 – 5 " x WOF strips

SEWING INSTRUCTIONS:

Trim two 5" border strips to 38 ½". Sew to the sides of the large background square. Press seams toward the border strips.

Piece together the remaining three 5" border strips. From this, cut two lengths 47 ½". Sew to the top and bottom of the background square. Press the seams toward the border strips.

Use the Summer of '51 appliqué templates from Page 87 and instructions on pages 16 and 17, and appliqué the design in each corner of the background, letting the design overlap the seam in the borders. Refer to the photo below.

When the appliqué is complete, press the piece gently from the back side.

Hazel's youngest brother Larry, aka Puz, with a sparkling clean face. Larry turned 10 in the summer of '51.

Layer the quilt top with the backing and batting, and quilt with the design of your choice. Use the aqua solid fabric for the binding.

Web extra: For the quilting design for the Summer of '51 Tablecloth, go to hazelsdiary.wordpress.com.

Summer of '51 Embroidered Dresser Scarf

Finished size: 16" x 42"
Made by Shelly Pagliai

Hazel's mother, Mildred, never let a dresser go naked in her house. She had an extensive collection of dresser scarves from which to choose when covering the tops of every dresser the Hyde family owned. In honor of this family tradition, I created this embroidered version of a dresser scarf on a linen background, using a reduced-size version of the Summer of '51 appliqué as my embroidery design.

SUPPLY LIST

- ½ yard tan linen for background

- 1 yard ½" aqua rickrack for trim

- DMC embroidery floss, 1 skein each of the following colors:

    #604 Pink

    #321 Red

    #726 Yellow

    #721 Orange

    #959 Turquoise #1

    #964 Turquoise #2

    #702 Green #1

    #704 Green #2

CUTTING INSTRUCTIONS

From the linen, remove the selvage edges and cut a piece 17″ x 43″.

From the rickrack, cut 2 – 17″ lengths.

SEWING INSTRUCTIONS

Line a piece of rickrack up along one short end of the linen piece 3 ½″ in from the edge. Stitch the rickrack in place. Repeat on the other end of the linen piece with the remaining piece of rickrack.

Press under ¼″ on all edges of the linen piece, then press under again ¼″. Stitch this folded edge in place around the entire edge of the linen piece to make a neat, hemmed edge.

Use the diagram below for the design. Position the design 1″ in from the rickrack trim, so that the leaves that meet in the middle are about ½″ apart.

Trace the design onto the four corners of your linen piece.

The black lines on the diagram are the basic design.

The red lines denote the extra stitches I did.

Embroider the design, using any colors and stitches you would like. Fill in the flowers and leaves as much as you want.

I used these stitches: outline stitch, backstitch, straight stitch, lazy daisy, French knots and running stitch.

All the black lines on the diagram were done with the outline stitch.

In the large flower centers, I used running stitch, outline stitch and a French knot. In the large flower petals, I used backstitch with French knots in between the lines of backstitch and outline stitch.

In the large leaves, I used backstitch for the vein up through the middle, filled in with straight stitches. In the small leaves, I used backstitch in the centers and two French knots on each side, with a lazy daisy at the point of the center stitching.

Stars Over Missouri Quilt

Finished size: 84" x 84"
Made by Shelly Pagliai

For the very first block of the Hazel's Diary quilt, I chose the traditional Missouri Star block as my base block for a couple of reasons. Hazel was born and raised and lived her entire life in Missouri. The one and only time she mentions quilting in the diary, she wrote, "I made 11 star quilt blocks. Making a quilt." So Missouri Star seemed a logical choice, and I wanted to include it in the quilt somehow.

The traditional Missouri Star block is also one of my all-time favorite quilt blocks, so I decided to use lots of them in two sizes to make this medallion-style quilt that features bright colors, polka dots and some happy appliqué that is simple to do.

For the focal print centers in my blocks, I used a vintage print that I picked up at a rummage sale – a print that might possibly have been something Hazel could have had in her own stash. Pulling colors from that print, I chose yellows and reds in several different polka dot styles, and even a solid yellow made its way in. To complete my palette, I chose a modern turquoise print that went with them all. Although I made my quilt with a controlled color palette, it still contains quite a variety of fabrics. I think it would make a wonderful scrappy quilt.

SUPPLY LIST

- 5¼ yards white solid for the background

- 1¼ yards multicolored focal print with navy, red, yellow and aqua for the block centers

- Various yellow polka dot, solid or tone-on-tone fabrics to equal 1⅝ yards for the triangles around the center square

- 1¾ yard turquoise print for the inner color of the star points

- Various red polka dot fabrics to equal 1¾ yards for the outer color of the star points

These amounts will leave you with enough leftovers to use for the appliqué pieces.

- ¾ yard for binding

- 7¾ yards for backing (44/45") or 2½ yards of 90"-wide backing

ASSEMBLY INSTRUCTIONS

The quilt is put together from the center outward. You can either add the appliqué to each inner border section as you go, or wait until you have the entire quilt assembled and then do the appliqué, whichever you prefer.

12" BLOCK

From the white background fabric, cut:

- 1 – 7 ¼" square – Cut the square from corner to corner twice on the diagonal to make 4 triangles. (A1)
- 4 – 3 ½" squares (A3)
- From the focal print fabric, cut:
- 1 – 4 ¾" square (A2)
- From a yellow fabric, cut:
- 2 – 3 ⅞" squares – Cut the squares in half on the diagonal to make 4 triangles. (B1)

From the turquoise print, cut:

- 2 – 4 ¼" squares – Cut the squares from corner to corner twice on the diagonal to make 8 triangles. (C1)

From a red polka dot print, cut:

- 2 – 4 ¼" squares – Cut the squares from corner to corner twice on the diagonal to make 8 triangles. (D1)

Follow the instructions on pages 43 and 44 for making the Missouri Farm Life block. Make 28 12" finished blocks.

6" BLOCK

From the white background fabric, cut:

- 1 – 4 ¼" square – Cut the square from corner to corner twice on the diagonal to make 4 triangles. (A1)
- 4 – 2" squares (A3)
- From the focal print fabric, cut:
- 1 – 2 ⅝" square (A2)
- From a yellow fabric, cut:
- 2 – 2 ⅜" squares – Cut the squares in half on the diagonal to make 4 triangles. (B1)

From the turquoise print, cut:

- 2 – 2 ¾" squares – Cut the squares from corner to corner twice on the diagonal to make 8 triangles. (C1)

From a red polka dot print, cut:

- 2 – 2 ¾" squares – Cut the squares from corner to corner twice on the diagonal to make 8 triangles. (D1)

Follow the instructions on pages 43 and 44 for making the Missouri Farm Life block. Make 28 6" finished blocks.

QUILT ASSEMBLY

Sew four of the 12" blocks together as shown to make the center of the quilt.

From the white background fabric, cut:

- 10 – 6 ½" x WOF strips

Trim two 6 ½" background strips to 24 ½". Sew one to each side of the center section, pressing seams toward the strips.

Trim two 6 ½" background strips to 36 ½". Sew to the top and bottom of the center section, again pressing seams toward the strips.

This portion of the quilt should now measure 36 ½".

For the next round, sew the 6" star blocks into two rows of six blocks each, and two rows of 8 blocks each.

Sew the rows of six blocks onto the sides of the quilt center. Press seams toward the appliqué background.

Sew the rows of eight blocks to the top and bottom, again pressing seams toward the appliqué background.

Piece six 6 ½" background strips together to make one long strip. From this, cut two lengths 48 ½".

Sew a 48 ½" background strip to each side of the quilt, pressing seams toward the strips.

From the long 6 ½" background strip, cut two lengths 60 ½". Sew to the top and bottom, again pressing seams toward the strips.

The quilt should now measure 60 ½".

Sew the remaining 12" finished blocks into two rows of five blocks each, and two rows of seven blocks each.

Sew the rows of five blocks onto the sides of the quilt, pressing seams toward the appliqué background. Sew the rows of seven blocks to the top and bottom, again pressing seams toward the appliqué background.

Using the appliqué templates on Page 94, cut the appliqué pieces from various leftover prints as follows:

For the inner appliqué border:
- 4 large stars
- 8 medium stars
- 8 small stars
- 16 large circles
- 16 small circles

For the outer appliqué border:
- 8 large stars
- 16 medium stars
- 16 small stars
- 24 large circles
- 24 small circles

Using the quilt photo as a placement guide, arrange the appliqué pieces onto the background sections, and appliqué them in place using your favorite appliqué method.

APPLIQUÉ TEMPLATES ON PAGE 95

Hazel, freshman year
of high school

This is the vintage fabric I picked up at a rummage sale and used as the focal print in my blocks. I used the colors from this fabric to pick the coordinating fabrics.

74

Happily Ever After Quilt

Finished size: 66" x 78"
Made by Shelly Pagliai

By the time Hazel's senior year of high school was winding down, she was engaged and happily looking forward to becoming a wife and mother. She was busy making items for her hope chest, wrapping up her final year of high school and looking forward to beginning wedding planning in the summer of 1954.

The entire Hyde family took a 16-day vacation in August, driving up into South Dakota, then through Wyoming, Montana and Idaho, on their way to Washington state to visit Mildred's sister, Esther. They took another route home, sightseeing through Oregon, California, Nevada, Utah, Colorado and Kansas. It was the last family vacation the five of them went on together, because Hazel was married in October.

Hazel and Dale began their married life in a little 5-room rented farmhouse. They wanted nothing more than to live happily ever after.

This quilt uses the Domestic Bliss block from the Hazel's Diary quilt, without the appliqué. This block design is loosely based on the traditional block called Single Wedding Ring. It's a straight setting with no sashing and plain borders. A variety of fabrics makes it scrappy, giving it a nice retro, '50s feel.

SUPPLY LIST

- 15 fat quarters of assorted prints in various colors or the equivalent in scraps for blocks.

- 2 yards background fabric for blocks and border

- ⅝ yard for binding

- 5 yards for backing (44/45") or 2 yards of 90"-wide backing

ASSEMBLY INSTRUCTIONS

Using the instructions for the Domestic Bliss block on pages 39-41, make 30 12" blocks.

Note: These blocks don't need the frames, so you do not have to cut pieces A6 and A7.

From the background fabric, cut:

* 8 – 3 1/2" x WOF strips for the outer borders.

Place the blocks in 6 rows of 5 blocks each, in an arrangement that you like.

Sew the blocks together in rows, then sew the rows together to complete the quilt center.

Sew the 3 1/2" border strips together in pairs to make 4 longer strips.

From two of these strips, cut lengths of 72 1/2". Sew these to the sides of the quilt top, pressing the seams toward the strips.

From the two remaining strips, cut lengths of 66 1/2". Sew these to the top and bottom of the quilt, again pressing the seams toward the strips.

Hazel's senior portrait,
taken Oct. 21, 1953.

Best. Christmas. Ever. Quilt

Finished size: 56" x 56"
Made by Shelly Pagliai

Hazel declared on Christmas Day 1952, "This is the best Christmas ever" – and I knew right away that I wanted to incorporate the traditional Christmas Star block into my Hazel's Diary quilt. I chose to use it again to make a medallion-style quilt that works as a bed topper or a table topper or a Christmas wall hanging.

Table linens and fabrics from the early 1950s sometimes use very unexpected color combinations, such as bright red horses or gray tulips. So when I came across black and gray Christmas fabric, I decided to make a Christmas quilt with an unexpected color combination.

The blocks themselves don't have any appliqué on them – I moved the appliqué into the center triangles to accent the medallion setting.

SUPPLY LIST

- 3 yards white solid background fabric for blocks, setting triangles and borders

- ⅓ yard of a focal print for the block centers

- ½ yard each of two different reds for blocks and appliqué

- 1 fat quarter of black for blocks and stems

- ½ yard of black print for blocks and appliqué

- ½ yard for binding

- 3 ½ yards for backing (44/45") or 1 ¾ yards of 90"-wide backing

ASSEMBLY INSTRUCTIONS

Using the instructions for the Best. Christmas. Ever. block on pages 32 and 33, make 13 –12" finished blocks.

Note: You don't need to cut pieces A5 and A6 because these blocks are not framed. Piece A1 gets cut from the focal fabric.

CUTTING INSTRUCTIONS:

From background fabric, cut:

- 2 –18" squares
- Cut these squares in half once on the diagonal to make 4 setting triangles
- 6 – 4 ½" x WOF from the background fabric strips for border

From the binding fabric, cut:

- 6 – 2 ¼" x WOF strips

SETTING ASSEMBLY:

To make the center medallion, sew a large background triangle to two opposite sides of one of the 12" blocks. To get them positioned correctly, locate the center point of the long side of the triangle and match it up with the center point of the side of the block. Press seams toward the triangles. Trim the edges of the triangles even with the edges of the block, as shown.

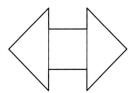 

Sew the two remaining triangles to the other two sides. Press seams toward the triangles.

Make sure this unit measures 24 ½" square, trimming if necessary.

Sew the remaining finished 12" pieced blocks into two rows of two blocks each, and two rows of 4 blocks each.

Sew the two-block rows to the sides of the quilt top, pressing seams toward the background fabric.

Sew the four-block rows to the top and bottom, pressing seams toward the background fabric.

ADDING THE BORDERS:

Piece three of the 4 ½" border strips together to make one long strip. From this, cut two lengths 48 ½". Add these strips to the sides of the quilt.

Piece three more 4 ½" strips together and from it, cut two lengths 56 ½". Add these to the top and bottom of the quilt.

Using the appliqué templates on pages 91 and 95, appliqué the poinsettia design on each corner around the center medallion using your preferred method of applique.

APPLIQUÉ TEMPLATES ON PAGE 96

Fancy Farm Girl Quilt

Finished size: 80" x 92"
Made by Shelly Pagliai

Hazel loved fashion and sewed a lot of her own clothing. She made several of her formal gowns for school events. She also made a wool suit and a blouse for traveling on her honeymoon. She was aware of the popular colors and fabrics of the time and was constantly changing her hairstyle to keep up with all the latest trends. And folks dressed up for nearly any occasion – boys wore trousers, and girls wore dresses and skirts.

March 16, 1954

Got my Italian hair cut & perm. today. I don't care for it – but maybe it'll be better when it losens up. I hope so. Stayed home tonite. Got my history (homework). 10 of us girls go to Macon tomorrow.

May 28, 1954

Dale came up tonite & we went to the Drive-in. I ironed this aft. & also finished my petticoat too. I love it – Its made out of an old sheet. Bye

I chose my favorite block from the main quilt, Fancy Farm Girl, and simply repeated it to make a fabulously scrappy quilt with a pieced border that extends the block design out to the edges.

I used a wide assortment of fabrics that represent the colors that were popular when Hazel was in high school and put them all together with a background fabric that resembles newspaper pages as they looked in the early 1950s. It has the most wonderful vintage look to it, and is one of my favorite quilts ever.

This quilt is meant to be busy and scrappy, and each block is different. The more fabrics you include, the better, so choose a large variety, and have fun with it.

SUPPLY LIST

- 5 ¼ yards background fabric for blocks and borders

- Assorted prints to equal 5 ¾ yards for blocks and borders

- ¾ yard for binding

- 7 ⅓ yards for backing (44/45") or 2 ½ yards of 108"-wide backing

PIECED BLOCK

From background, cut:

- 1 – 5 1/4" square – Cut the square in half twice on the diagonal to make a total of 4 triangles. (A1)
- 4 – 2 7/8" squares – Draw a diagonal line on the reverse side of these squares with a marking pencil. (A3)
- 8 – 2 1/2" squares (A4)

From assorted prints, cut:

- 1 – 3 3/8" square (A2)
- 2 – 2 7/8" squares – Cut these squares in half on the diagonal to make a total of 4 triangles. (B1)
- 3 – 5 1/4" squares – Cut the squares in half twice on the diagonal to make a total of 12 triangles. (C1 and D1) Two of the squares have to be from the same print, while the third is from a different print.
- 4 – 2 7/8" squares (E1)

BORDER UNITS

From background fabric, cut:

- 56 – 2 7/8" squares – Draw a diagonal line on the reverse side of these squares with a marking pencil. (A3)
- 112 – 2 1/2" squares (A4)

From assorted prints, cut:

- 56 – 2 7/8" squares (E1)

SETTING ASSEMBLY:

Arrange the blocks in 7 rows of 6 blocks, in an arrangement that suits you.

Sew them together to complete the quilt's center.

To make the borders, sew the border units and background squares into units as shown. Make certain that you have them turned correctly when you sew them together. Make 26 of these units. You should have four triangle–square units left over. These are for the corners.

Sew the border sections into two rows of 6 sections and two rows of 7 sections, as shown. Again, make sure that you have them turned correctly before stitching them together.

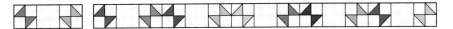

Sew the rows of 7 sections to the sides of the quilt, making sure you have them turned correctly so that the border units form a star when matched up against the blocks.

Hazel's cousin, Peggy Rector, with a headful of curls, bottle-feeds a lamb while wearing a dress and patent leather Mary Janes. Now that's a fancy farm girl!

To each end of the remaining border strips, sew one of the leftover triangle square units, making sure they are turned as shown.

Sew these to the top and bottom of the quilt, once again paying close attention to the orientation of the strips so that the units form stars where they join the blocks.

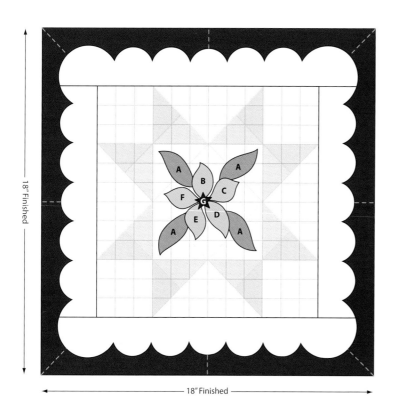

**HAZEL'S DIARY QUILT, BLOCK 1:
MISSOURI FARM LIFE**

18" Finished

18" Finished

Each square = 1 inch

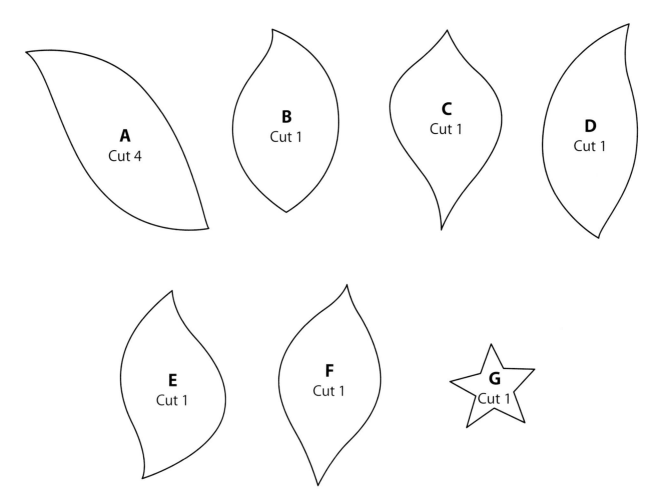

A
Cut 4

B
Cut 1

C
Cut 1

D
Cut 1

E
Cut 1

F
Cut 1

G
Cut 1

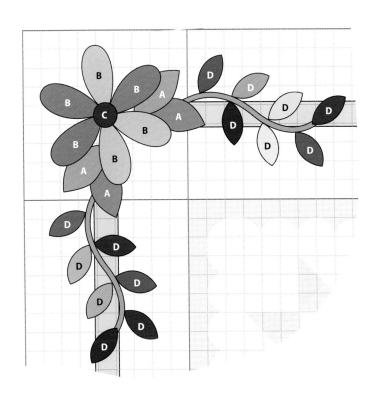

Each square = 1 inch

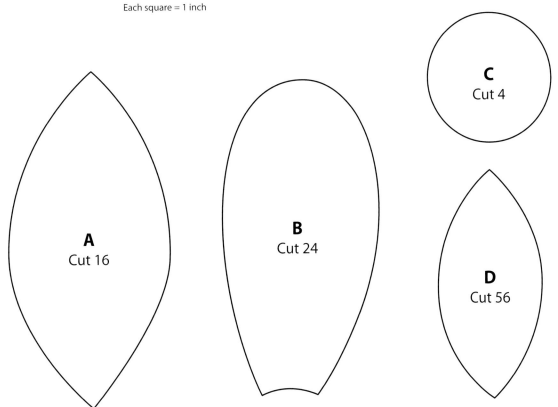

C
Cut 4

A
Cut 16

B
Cut 24

D
Cut 56

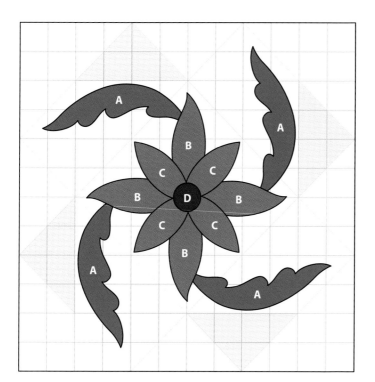

Each square = 1 inch

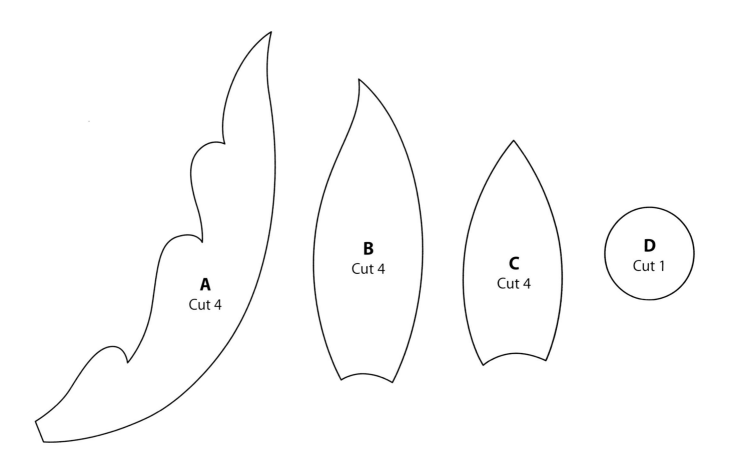

A
Cut 4

B
Cut 4

C
Cut 4

D
Cut 1

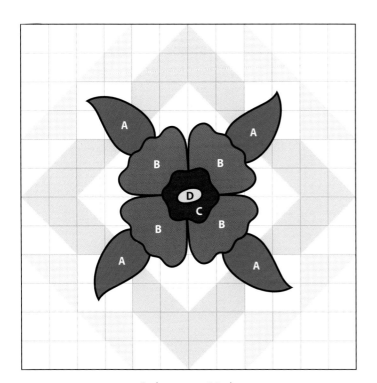

Each square = 1 inch

HAZEL'S DIARY QUILT, BLOCK 4:
COAL MINER'S GRAND-DAUGHTER

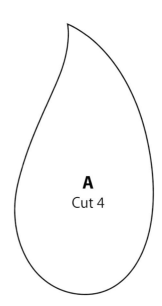

A
Cut 4

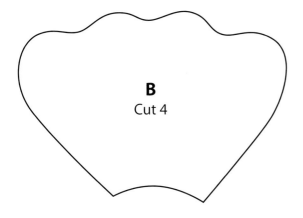

B
Cut 4

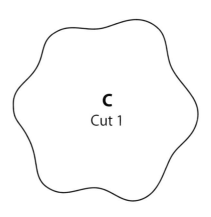

C
Cut 1

D
Cut 1

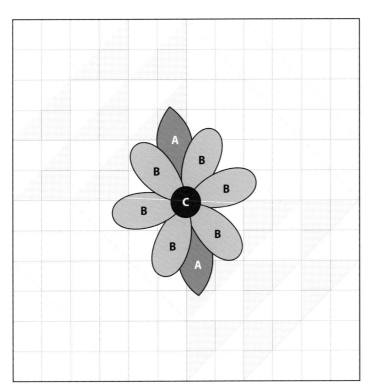

Each square = 1 inch

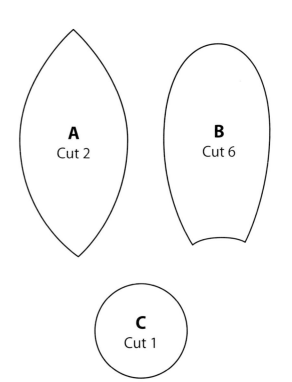

A
Cut 2

B
Cut 6

C
Cut 1

HAZEL'S DIARY QUILT, BLOCK 6:
BEST. CHRISTMAS. EVER.

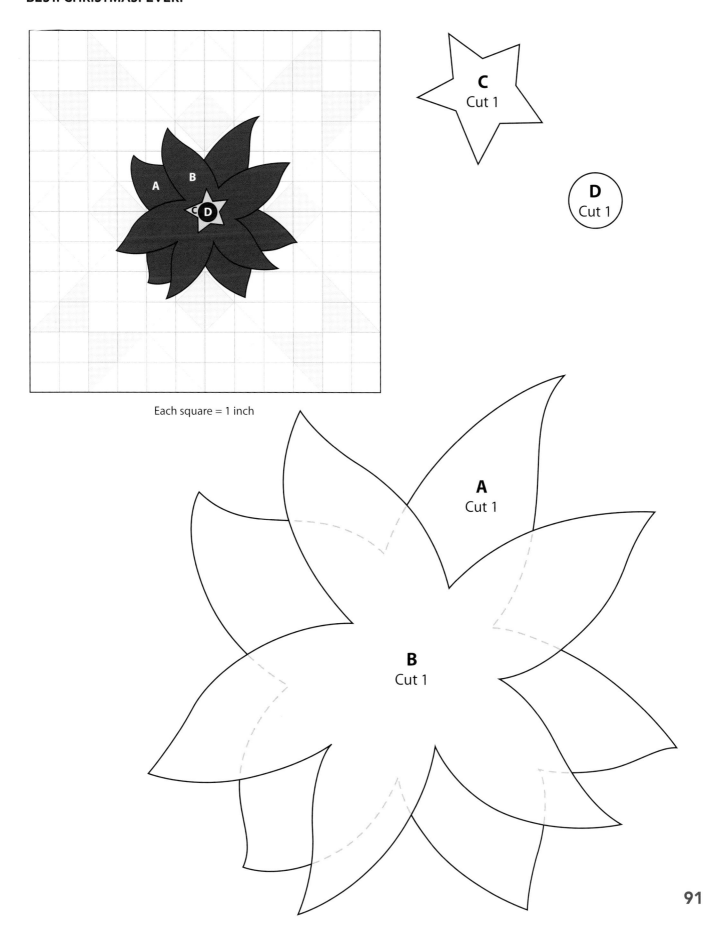

Each square = 1 inch

C
Cut 1

D
Cut 1

A
Cut 1

B
Cut 1

Each square = 1 inch

HAZEL'S DIARY QUILT, BLOCK 7:
AUNT RUBY'S CHOICE

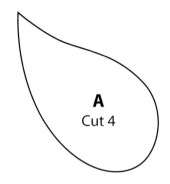

A
Cut 4

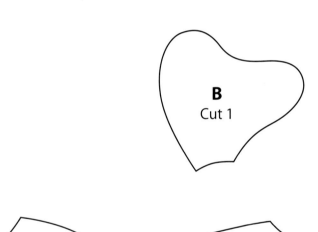

B
Cut 1

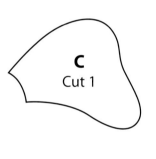

C
Cut 1

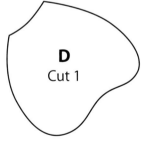

D
Cut 1

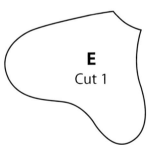

E
Cut 1

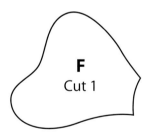

F
Cut 1

G
Cut 1

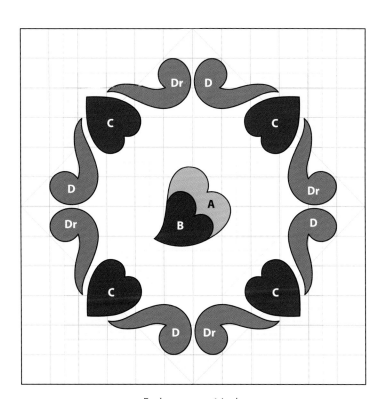

Each square = 1 inch

HAZEL'S DIARY QUILT, BLOCK 8:
DOMESTIC BLISS

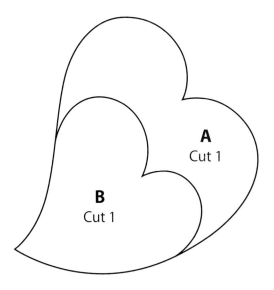

A
Cut 1

B
Cut 1

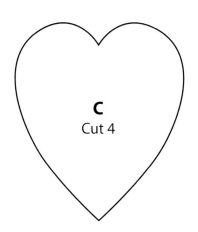

C
Cut 4

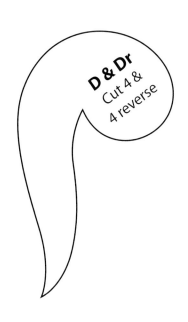

D & Dr
Cut 4 &
4 reverse

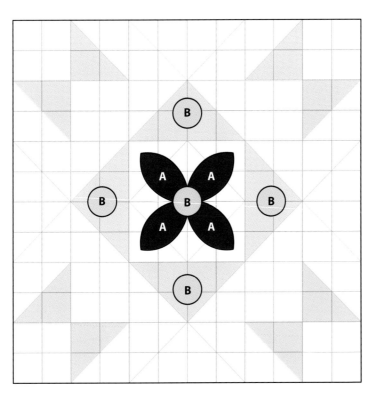

Each square = 1 inch

HAZEL'S DIARY QUILT, BLOCK 9: FANCY FARM GIRL

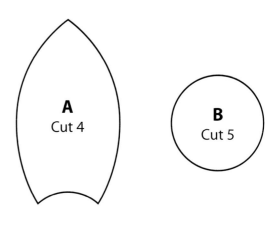

A
Cut 4

B
Cut 5

HAZEL'S DIARY QUILT, BLOCK 10: FAIR WEATHER

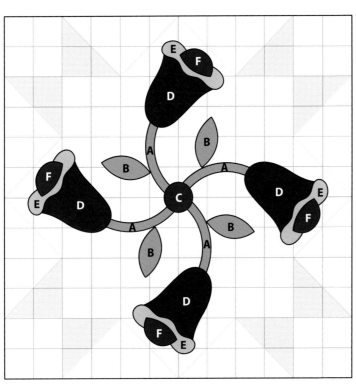

Each square = 1 inch

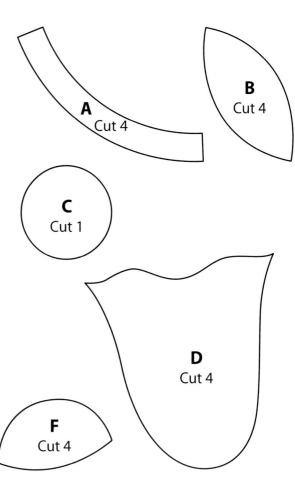

A
Cut 4

B
Cut 4

C
Cut 1

D
Cut 4

F
Cut 4

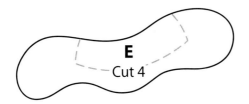

E
Cut 4

1″ square
for gauge

BEST. CHRISTMAS. EVER.

SEE PAGE 91 FOR THE POINSETTIA TEMPLATES.

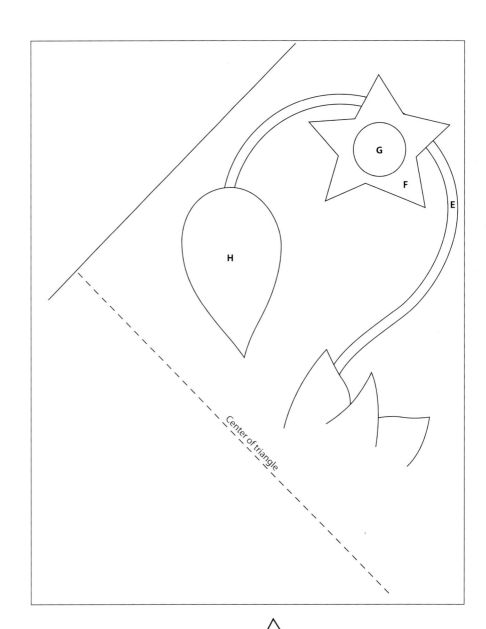

1" square for gauge

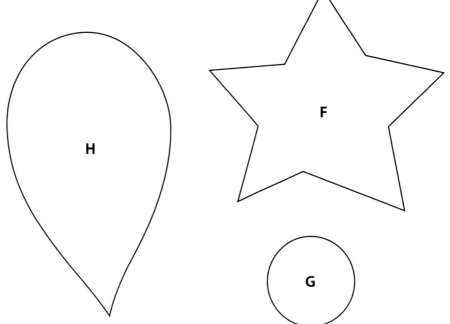